GO BIG
AND
STAY HOME

Connect, Refer, Create,
Your Road to Riches

By Tracie Hasse
Ambassador of Quality Connections
& Strategic Alliances

Foreword By Peggy McColl
Dynamic Destinies, Inc.

authorHOUSE®

AuthorHouse™
1663 Liberty Drive
Bloomington, IN 47403
www.authorhouse.com
Phone: 1 (800) 839-8640

Published by AuthorHouse   08/16/2016

ISBN: 978-1-5246-1957-2 (sc)
ISBN: 978-1-5246-1956-5 (e)

Library of Congress Control Number: 2016911960

Print information available on the last page.

This book is printed on acid-free paper.

Author Contact Information:

Tracie Hasse
Phone: (858) 356-2208
Address: 1155 Camino Del Mar, #123, Del Mar, CA 92014

Email: tracie@traciehasse.com
LinkedIn URL: www.linkedin.com/in/traciehasse
*Note in Subject line: *Go Big AND Stay Home*

Book Website: *www.GoBigANDStayHomeBook.com*

Book Cover by Reed Reppa and Design by Tracie Hasse.

Dedication

I am forever grateful to Reed, my fiancé, for his deep love, endless patience, and enduring support of me. Infinite love and gratitude to Momma, Poppa, and Todd, my brother, for cheering me on from heaven, and Todd's life motto "Go Big Or Stay Home" that inspired me to write *Go Big AND Stay Home*.

Contents

Advance Praise For *Go Big AND Stay Home*

"Go Big & Stay Home is authentic, real, rich, and even...genius. Yes, genius. Tracie Hasse has taken vast concepts and presented them into easy, digestible, practical and useful tools that anyone can implement immediately to build a successful business and life. She has what I call, exceptional "RQ" (Relationship Quotient/ Intelligence) and this is clearly demonstrated throughout the book. From the very start, Tracie sets the stage for her readers and with each chapter, she releases gems of wisdom where the reader is left saying "I can do this!"
~Dr. Manna Ko, Manna For Life, Founder/CEO: Sought-after Speaker, Leadership Trainer and Business/Life Strategist; Author of 9 books including her recent Best Seller, "Made For More"

"Tracie Hasse is the ultimate connector and it shows on every page of her exciting new book. As a passionate fellow relationship marketer myself, I agree wholeheartedly with the principles Tracie outlines in Go Big AND Stay Home. Thing is, these principles and skills are totally learnable. Even if you get overwhelmed by social media platforms and tools or you come home from networking events with stacks of business cards that end up gathering dust on your desk, with a few simple shifts you can transform your online and offline networking into measurable results and profits. Tracie shows you how!"
~Mari Smith, Premier Facebook Business Development Expert & Author "The New Relationship Marketing", Forbes Top Ten Social Media Power Influencers, International Keynote Speaker Specializing in Relationship Marketing

"Tracie is a genius at connecting people and opportunities that are destined to make it big. She is a master networker and brings an energy of joy and success into every endeavor she touches and her enthusiasm is irresistibly contagious! You can count on her to help you develop your best inspirations and to connect them to your network of friends and colleagues in fun and exciting ways. Her new book, *Go Big AND Stay Home* brings together the best of successful collaboration and the latest methods of leveraging online networks to turbo-charge your business opportunities. I have been working with Tracie since 2005 and highly recommend her work - her new book is a treasure-trove of business networking wisdom!"
~Christopher Dilts, Co-Founder Right Source Digital, Inc., ThoughtLeaderTransformation.com and Co-Author of "The Handbook of High Performance Virtual Teams" McMillian

"In today's quickly changing digital landscape, Tracie's book *Go Big AND Stay Home* is particularly relevant. In so many instances, the necessity of putting in commuting and brick and mortar office hours are non-essential and can even be detrimental to a business! Learning to navigate this culture, and do it in a productive way can be the very thing that allows your business to prosper when other's fail. Read this book to harness the power of your relationships and social networking to build a powerful business from your home office or anywhere in the world!"
~Viveka von Rosen, LinkedIn Expert & Author: "LinkedIn Marketing: An Hour a Day", International Keynote Speaker, Forbes Top 20 Most Influential Women in Social Media

"Tracie, I am a firm believer in eating the same soup that you serve, which is what you are doing. Statistically, over 78% of everyone employed in Corporate America is unhappy with his or her job. With your book, you are the new pied-piper who is committed to helping individuals find their way to their dreams in an easy to follow fun way of sharing."
~Coach Ron Nash: Master Career Coach, LinkedIn Strategist, and Author, newest book "How to LinkedIn"

"Tracie is the **ultimate connecter and master influencer.** *Go Big AND Stay Home* will help you achieve any goals you want while having fun in the process!"
~Roberto Monaco, InfluenceOlogy.com "The Best Presentation, Public Speaking and Influence Program in the World"

"Tracie has done it, *Go Big AND Stay Home* is a book for conscious entrepreneurs that is full of wisdom, tips, strategies, and entertaining stories that all point you in the direction of business success. If you are going to read one book this year, make it this one."
~Ken D Foster, Business Strategist, Intuitive Mentor, Business Trainer, Speaker & Author "20 Minutes of Courage" in 2016, "Stars of Courage 501C3"

"Tracie is an amazing women, who not only walks her talk, she has now written a powerful book to guide others in doing the same."
~ Judy Ann Foster, Founder of Women's Wisdom

"Tracie is one of those few people I would call an "uber connector"….one that consistently is thinking about how to help others and making introductions that facilitate long lasting business relationships."
~ **David Michail, Metlawgroup, Media, Entertainment, and Technology Counsel**

"Bravo to Tracie Hasse and her new book *Go Big AND Stay Home*! What an inspiration to business owners and professionals who want to create a successful career <u>and</u> do it on their own terms. Tracie offers quick and easy ways -- both online and offline -- to nurture relationships, leverage your networks, and build a strong referral base to create the life and business of your dreams. Her passion for connecting to create more wealth and happiness in your life literally leaps off the page!"
~**Rebecca Massoud, Business Success Coach & Marketing Mentor; Founder, SHINE Because It's Your Time**

"Tracie is the ultimate "connector!" She is a master at putting people together so that everyone wins. We have specifically worked with her on our LinkedIn marketing and have seen great results from her expertise. We wish her all the best on the launch of her book and look forward to continuing our great relationship with her."
~ **Jeff & Tina Rogers, Brainstorm Success, "The Quit Whining, No Excuses, Get Busy Creating The Life You Love Coach!"**

"Since knowing Tracie, my life has been enriched in so many ways. She is a person of great knowledge and wisdom. She has been an inspiration and motivation that has helped me bring about my true passion in life and work. Our brainstorming sessions have not only been true "works of art" but, fun, uplifting and a driving force that has moved me forward whenever I am stuck. Not only can I count on my dear friend for these moments in my life but, I can't wait until we can get together again!"

~ Dr. Steven Ross, Consultant, International Speaker, Practitioner, President/ Co-Founder & Educator, Advanced Medical Academy, a subsidiary of The American College of Integrative and Functional Medicine; Author of "Curing The Cause and Preventing Disease, A New Approach to The Diagnosis and Treatment of Illness and Aging with Functional Diagnostic Medicine"

Foreword By Peggy McColl

New York Times Best-Selling Author, The Best
Seller Maker, Millionaire Author Maker
Author of 11 books including her recent
Best Seller, "Darn Easy"

The title of this book is brilliant…Go Big AND Stay Home. If that is something you would love to do, then you are in the right place and at the right time. There has never been a better time in history to run your own business from the comfort of your home. Tracie will show you how to have that experience be seamless and enjoyable while honoring your hearts' desire in business.

More than 20 years ago I was sparked with an idea to incorporate my own business and run it from the comfort of my home. The idea was fanned into flame and became a mission and became my life. And, from this, I created a profitable business that continues to grow positively in revenue, profit and reach.

Starting a business was not something that I was trained to do. My own parents were hard working and dedicated employees of other businesses and having a role model for entrepreneurship or guidance on what was required to start and build a business was not something that I was exposed to. In fact, my siblings and I were discouraged from continuing our education because my family didn't have the funds to support that desire. Nor were we encouraged to step out of the "norm" and pursue our passion by running our own business.

Now that I have created my own business, and have run my own business for more than twenty years, I feel grateful every single day. The benefits are endless. To wake up every single day and feel blessed to do meaningful work, serving and sharing people in the world who benefit from your knowledge, experience and wisdom is truly fulfilling. I also love and appreciate how having a successful business has a ripple affect and positively impacts those around you.

As Tracie will share with you in her wonderful book, it really doesn't matter where you come from, your education or your background, if you have the desire, you can create anything. Follow her guidance, suggestions, and recommendations, learn from her brilliance and most importantly … apply it. When you do, you will experience the positive side of having greater and greater success. My only wish for you, is total success while you are 'Going Big.'

Introduction

Moving to Las Vegas, Nevada at five years old felt scary and overwhelming for this small town girl who was born in Cody, Wyoming, with a population of 3,000. After the culture shock wore off, it took some time for me and my family to adjust to life in the big city. Our hearts longed for the safety net of friendships we were blessed with in Cody.

This is a story about a small town girl who grew up in the big city and embarked on an extraordinary life of self-discovery, in order to find her unique calling for helping others to succeed and prosper.

In Cody, it was safe for my brothers George and Todd, and my sister Mary and I to play outside with the neighbors. We all played together. Everyone knew each other. Todd and I being the youngest were always on a mission to keep up with our older sister and brother, Mary and George. We did the usual small town things kids did to have fun and play. We rode our bikes, enjoyed swinging on swings, and visiting our favorite neighbor, Seddi, to eat yummy goodies like spiced gumdrops. In the winter we spent our time on the ski slopes and our snow covered yard. We never worried about being safe. Everyone looked out for each other in our wonderful small town. Las Vegas didn't feel safe when I was a little girl who didn't know anyone.

I started kindergarten in the big city as the new kid. I was painfully shy and didn't have any friends. The thought of going to a new school in a brand new place was terrifying for me. My parents had to carry me across the street kicking and screaming, and force me to go to school. As soon as my parents dropped me off, my teacher would cart me off to the nurse's office because I wouldn't stop crying. The nurse tried to help and find out if there was anything wrong with me. There was. I was scared about being a stranger in a strange land. But the nurse couldn't help me with that. As tears rolled down my cheeks, I thought to myself, *I'm not sick, I'm afraid and I don't have any friends here.*

My Mom helped me through this troubled time with a book I came to cherish and appreciate. Momma read, *A Fun Day at Kindergarten*, to me every night at bedtime. I loved the book, because I got to sit on my Momma's lap, where I felt safe. It helped me make the transition into kindergarten.

Later in life, I asked my Momma, "How did I finally get over being so upset and stop hiding in the house when it was time to go to school?" She reminded me it was because I had finally made a friend. She said, "Once you made that one friend you were happy about going to school. It changed everything for you." Neither one of us remembered that one friends name, probably because I quickly made many more friends after that.

As the years passed, I discovered that making new friends was like breathing air and drinking water for me. I needed relationships to survive. Making friends was important to me. I enjoyed nurturing and growing relationships. It came naturally to me. Relationships made me happy. Eventually, they became the central theme to my life. I am starting this book with my story, in an effort to show how my special gift for relationship building eventually became my unique way of helping others get what they want out of life.

My parents were my greatest teachers who led by example. I learned about the importance of relationships and how essential it is to stay connected and in touch with the people you love and care about. They had friendships that stood the test of time and lasted a lifetime, 70 years and more!

I consider my friends to be earth angels sprinkled throughout my life. They consist of people I've known since I was born, as well as new friends who are kindred spirits I feel like I've known for many moons.

In the winter months, snow skiing was the highlight of our family bonding. We practically learned how to ski at the same time we learned how to walk. From the time we were toddlers, Mom and Dad taught us how to snow ski. We have so many fond memories as a family on ski trips, racing each other down the mountain, run after run, until the slopes closed down for the day. During the summer months, we shifted from the slopes to the swimming pool to escape the scorching Las Vegas desert heat. We were an outdoorsy family that enjoyed water sports such as competing on swim and dive teams. You couldn't get us out of the water. My sister Mary and I even did water ballet. We loved making new friends and staying active and healthy.

My Mom was a classical pianist who taught me how to play the piano when I was seven years old. I was a natural and loved it. I was curious and enjoyed the challenge of exploring new activities throughout my childhood. I loved life and wanted to try it all. When I was ten I discovered gymnastics and immersed myself in competing and making new lifetime friends, especially Kathy and Laurie who are still near and dear to my heart. By the age of twelve, I won the All-Around Champion Gymnast Award at the Nevada State Competition. But eventually, injuries cut my budding gymnastics career short. From Junior High to High

School, I enjoyed the fun and popularity of being a cheerleader, and songleader, which was a combination of cheerleading and dancing. I also had the usual teenager interests, such as crushes on boys, partying, dancing, growing up, and learning lessons about life, as I continued to explore new experiences and adventures to satisfy my insatiable curiosity.

As a senior in high school I had no idea what I wanted to study in college. So, I attended Career Days to find out. It was there that I discovered a fascinating new program being offered called Biomedical Engineering. I thought to myself, "Well, I love people and it would be so cool to be a Doctor." This new degree seemed like a thrilling new adventure to me, so I said, "Yes, I'll do it!" There were only two colleges offering the curriculum at the time. One of them was in Boston and the other one in Arizona. Since I lived in Las Vegas, Arizona State University made the most sense for my budget. So off to a college adventure I went!

My parents engrained in all four of us kids that it was important to go to college to continue our education. It was what was expected of us after high school, no questions asked. Both my parents are proud that all four of us kids became college graduates. We all worked our way through college, won scholarships, and were awarded grants to fund our college educations. We were all determined and ambitious as we prepared to become adults and make our way in life. We were in action.

Two years into my college studies, I discovered that chemistry and I didn't blend so well. You can't really be an effective doctor when you get queasy at the sight of blood and needles. But, college was fun so I stayed and eventually switched majors. I enjoyed the usual college activities. I went through sorority rush and became a Kappa Kappa Gamma. That helped boost my social life with formals and other fun events. I developed wonderful friendships during my sorority days that I still have today!

I was burning the candle at both ends. I studied and worked, socialized, danced and partied whenever I got the chance! Eventually, I burned out and thought to myself, *There has got to be another way. I can't keep this up.* I was ready for a change. Since most of my friends were Business majors, I noticed that they studied a fraction of the time I did as a pre-med student. I wanted more time to have fun with my friends. So I briefly considered switching my major to Business.

I was blessed to have my dear friend "Rager Ron" in my life. Little did he know he was the catalyst for a critical shift in my college studies, when he suggested I meet with his college advisor Greg to check out Construction Engineering and Management. Now this was a major I never would have thought to consider. I thought construction was for men. How would this major work for me, a woman? It was just the beginning of my journey.

Now, it is an amusing part of my story I am proud to tell. I was open to possibilities, and with that came opportunities. I discovered that the Construction Engineering curriculum was a combination of Business and Engineering. That intrigued me. I learned about all the facets of the construction industry from engineering to the business side including: land development and physics, to budgeting, accounting, planning, scheduling, and negotiating contracts. I learned it all and loved it. It turned out I had a knack for it.

Go Big AND Stay Home

So I did it. I graduated with a Bachelor of Science Degree in Construction Engineering & Management, from Arizona State University in December 1988. Halleluiah! It ended up being a path that opened up many exciting career opportunities for me.

Before I graduated, I got to spend my last summer break with my sister Mary in Newport Beach, California. We had a blast. I fell in love with California and knew it would eventually be my home. During that summer, my bold and fearless networking lead to my first internship. That is when the spark of my superpower began. Networking has opened so many doors of opportunity for me throughout my life.

That internship opened other doors for me after I graduated. One such door was the chance to be a Project Engineer on the John Wayne Airport Terminal Building Project, in Irvine, California. Wow! I was on my way. It was so exciting and interesting. I was proud to hear my niece and nephews brag about their aunt who built the John Wayne Airport.

Through hard work and continuing to network and build relationships, more exciting career opportunities came my way. I was elated when The Walt Disney Company recruited me. As a result of my strong work ethic and relationship skills, I became an integral part of the Walt Disney Construction & Engineering Team. I got to work on the Disneyland Park and Hotel Renovation projects in Anaheim, California. That was a lot of hard work but very rewarding.

Working on the Walt Disney Team set the bar high for me and instilled a strong work ethic that has served me well throughout my work history. They appreciated my contributions, work ethic, and positive energy.

Introduction

While working at Disneyland Park in Anaheim, I learned so much about what it takes to maintain, innovate and expand the world-renowned Disneyland Park. I understood why they were so famous in the business world. At that time, they were the business system everyone wanted to copy and implement. They had developed a system for success that was getting astounding results. I was proud to be a part of it.

As employees, we received the coolest perks. The *Silver Pass* benefit gave me tons of free passes to share with whoever I wanted. Needless to say, it made me quite popular with my family and friends. One of my favorite perks was when Disney would close the park to the public to host holiday parties for employees only. They were very generous in how they appreciated their employees.

I am grateful for my years at Disney. I created many fond memories and cherished friendships as a result of being part of *The Orange Team* in the Construction & Engineering Division. I learned a lot from our fearless team leader Lynn. She was an incredible inspiration, a great leader, and brilliant business woman.

With an insatiable hunger to learn more about what made Disney thrive and become so successful, I pursued an opportunity with Disney Development, in Burbank, California. Even though I was already a Walt Disney Employee, it took eight interviews before I was offered the position. I moved from Newport Beach to Pasadena to be closer to work.

As a Project Manager for Tenant Improvement projects, I was responsible for overseeing the build-out of office spaces in the high-rises the Walt Disney Company owned and managed. I got to work side-by-side with one some of the best Architects and Engineers in the world on the Walt Disney Imagineering Building project. I was thrilled! It was an exciting time for me working for the Walt Disney Company. I felt like I had won the lottery.

Eventually though, as I came up for air and started doing some soul-searching, I began to question whether or not Construction Engineering was really the right fit for me. It was very stressful and I was working really long hours. Even though I learned a lot and was proud to be working at the Walt Disney Company, when I was honest with myself I realized I wasn't passionate about the work itself. Something was missing for me. It was time to move on and figure out what was next.

Luckily, I had many friends and family members in Sales. Networking with all the relationships I had nurtured over the years helped me make a career transition into sales. As a people person, sales was a good fit for me.

My dear friend Suzanne showed me what was possible as a sales professional when she invited me on a trip she had won as a result of achieving her sales goals. During that trip, Suzanne introduced me to her coworker Adrienne. Adrienne had previously worked at Kodak. She helped me make a connection with her previous manager at Kodak in New York. He referred me to the Los Angeles office and helped me get an interview. Two weeks later, I resigned from Walt Disney and started my sales career working for Kodak.

I kicked off my sales career with an intense three-month sales training boot camp. The last two months of the boot camp tested my will and determination, as I froze my toosh off in the harsh winter of Rochester, New York. Eventually, I made it to Graduation day. I was ecstatic when they announced my sales territory was going to be Beverly Hills west to Santa Monica! I was happy to move back to my beloved Southern California and get settled into Hermosa Beach to launch my new career and life.

I was in my element. A passion ignited in me as I met new people and got to expand my network of fabulous friendships. I had a circle of friends I could trust who supported my success. We had many cold calling adventures in the high rises of Beverly Hills.

In sales if you aren't getting kicked out of buildings you aren't trying hard enough. I learned a lot about what it took to be successful in sales. I learned to ride the waves of success and failure as I thrived on the elation of closing a deal and survived the rejection of all the "No's" I had to endure. The rewards of success were worth it. Winning paid trips as a result of meeting my sales goals was such a thrill for me. I was happy and thriving in my new lifestyle. But then something happened that changed me forever.

My brother Todd was killed suddenly. I was devastated. I couldn't believe it. I was there when it happened. We were walking across a street together with Bob, my crush at the time. We were only a few steps apart when the car hit Todd. We never saw it coming. It could have been me or Bob. It came out of nowhere. Todd was ripped from my life in an instant.

It was so difficult for me to grasp the magnitude of Todd's death because he had escaped it so many times before in his dare-devil lifestyle. He had been living under a cloud with a silver-lining his whole life. He had been so fearless as he explored many adventures in his short life. It was surreal to me that he wasn't with us any longer.

Todd was so full of life. How could he be dead? He lived life to the fullest in every single experience and day that he was alive as he leaped from one fearless feat to another. He lived by his mantra, "Go Big or Stay Home!"

After he graduated from college, just six short years before his death, he lived in Lake Tahoe where he spent his time outdoors and active as much as possible playing golf, mountain biking, and skiing. He called Lake Tahoe his "Heaven on Earth." He was a thrill-seeker, taking flight like an eagle as he soared off fifty-foot drops no one else would dare go near. He nailed the landing every time. I was in awe of his courage and bravery. I was amazed at his luck as he cheated death many times, walking away from car accidents where the car was totaled and he barely had a scratch on him. I was heartbroken when his luck ran out.

Todd's death rattled my cage. It catapulted me onto a spiritual journey that caused me to take a deeper look at my life. I searched for answers that never came, wondering why it wasn't me who got hit by that car. It caused me to inquire about the deeper meaning of life. I realized life would never be the same for me.

All the love, support, and prayers of all the earth angels in my life helped me cope and make it through the worst time of my life. My friend Craig said to me, "Tracie, you never get over it, you get on with it."

Twenty years have passed since Todd's death. I'm surprised at how much of an emotional impact it still has on me today, as tears soak the page I am writing these words upon. Todd's death has taught me about grief and letting go. It has prepared me for dealing with loss in life. My friendship with Bob didn't last much longer after Todd died. I had lost my two best friends. I had to learn how to cope and move on.

Several months later, my four-year old nephew ran into my brother George and his wife's bedroom one morning waking them up. He was excited as he told them, "Mom, Dad, Uncle Todd came to me last night! He was so bright I could barely look at him. He said he loves us all very much and he's getting a lot of skiing and golfing in!" Wow, can you imagine a message from beyond filtered through a four year old? That's probably because they haven't developed any mental blocks to such communications. They are so innocent and receptive. We were stunned and grateful.

Shortly after Todd said "hi" through my sweet little nephew, I realized, during a healing session with a medical intuitive counselor, that Todd wasn't gone because he wasn't outside of me. He would live eternally through me, in my heart and soul. He is with me now, as I write these words. This belief comforts me even today, over 20 years later. It helped me heal my grief so I could move on. It was time to live my life more fully for both me and Todd.

I've discovered over the course of my life that my successes are attributed to my willingness and ability to move through difficult times and challenges, to live life more fully. The pain of loss has served to deepen my love of life to live it with more appreciation. I've been blessed with angels who watch over me from heaven, as well as all the earth angels, family, friends, divine healers, coaches, mentors, coworkers, and clients who surround me and enrich my life. My network of relationships nurtures and energizes me, infusing me with an excitement about living life.

It is because of my relationships and work ethic that I have landed such spectacular jobs throughout my amazing career. Friends recruited me because of the relationships I've nurtured with them, which has served me well. I'm grateful to my network for supporting me in achieving my ongoing goals and dreams.

My growing network kept me working and growing professionally and personally. As I grieved over my brother's death, I had to keep on living life and continue onward during my career transitions in spite of the grief.

My close friend Stephen offered me a career opportunity I couldn't refuse when he recruited me as his, Western Region Business Development Director, for RareMedium.com, at the Los Angeles office. It was an exhilarating time for me to be part of the "dot-com boom" from 1999-2000. I learned new skills and gained wisdom and experience because of Stephen's faith in me.

Then that bubble burst when the dot-com industry crashed while my personal life was crashing and burning too. I needed to escape an abusive relationship and find a new career. I was ready to start the next chapter of my life and career. Sometimes bad things make good things happen. When faced with life challenges, I've come to know there are blessings and lessons through these difficult times. It was during this time I discovered San Diego. Before I knew it, I was able to move to my happily-ever-after home of San Diego, California, to start anew. I was ready for a more peaceful, laid-back, lifestyle after years of excitement living and working in the fast lane of Los Angeles.

Introduction

When I moved to San Diego, I discovered the Tony Robbins Company. I was ready to learn something new and start over. I wrote a letter to Human Resources explaining why they should hire me. I received a call, interviewed, and got hired! I spent the next eight months working for Tony Robbins doing inside sales. I learned so much from that experience. Working for Tony Robbins was like going through an intense university about life. It was there, that I discovered how powerful the simple practice of writing my thoughts, goals, and dreams down on paper can be. To see it in black and white makes it real.

I learned a lot of new skills and success principles that I'm grateful for and use today. I also learned something important about myself that I hadn't been aware of before. Being an inside sales rep on the phone all day stuck in an office wasn't a good fit for me. I felt disconnected being on the phone and never meeting these people I was talking with. The face-to-face connections are what fuel my fire coupled with the phone interaction.

My Tony Robbins coach, Gary helped me gain clarity as he took me through a coaching process that asked a lot of key questions. I wrote down my answers that gave me clarity on my dream career lifestyle. I discovered that it was essential for me to connect with people in-person in addition to on the phone. I needed that human contact up-close and in-person. Connecting with people face-to-face energized and inspired me. It was essential to my success and well-being. Sitting in a cubicle relentlessly dialing for dollars on the phone wasn't. It was time to move on to the next opportunity. The question became, did my dream career exist?

I called the first person on my list of resources, my friend Connie at Heritage Escrow to explore the possibility of joining the company's sales team. As it turned out, the timing was very synchronistic. They had just fired one of their Sales Executives earlier that day. I landed an interview and started my new career with them the following week at their Escondido office. Eight months later, the Rancho Santa Fe office was hiring. They invited me to interview. I was hired. I transferred to my new *home away from home* at the Rancho Santa Fe office where I thrived for eight years. It was the perfect job for me. I was getting paid to build relationships and connect people. I thrived, succeeded, and prospered. My career was back on track and life was good. I was happy. I didn't think it could get any better, until something unexpected and wonderful happened.

In August 2006, I met Reed. From our first date, we started building our relationship. Reed and I have a deep and unexplainable soul connection that continues to grow stronger every day. External challenges over the years have strengthened our bond. While we are soul mates, we've endured our share of challenges. For many years, we tolerated the challenges of a long distance relationship due to circumstance beyond our control.

A few months after we met, Reed moved to Buenos Aires, Argentina, to pursue his dream to learn Spanish and invest in real estate there. I enjoyed traveling with him from Buenos Aires throughout the Patagonia region to the southern tip of Argentina. Reed's Buenos Aires adventures were cut short when he received an urgent call that his father was fighting for his life in a hospital in New York City. He had a massive heart attack and his gall bladder had exploded. In 24-hours, Reed moved his life from Buenos Aires to New York to be by his father's side. He was all his father had. His mother had passed away a few years earlier.

Reed spent the next several years taking care of his father. He helped him learn how to eat, drink, and walk again. That was a challenging time for all of us. In spite of it, Reed and I grew closer.

I flew out to New York every chance I got to be by Reed's side. It was an emotional rollercoaster ride. When his father would recover from one thing then something else with his health would go sideways. He endured colon cancer, then pneumonia. Old age was taking its toll. We wanted to help more, but all the trips back and forth between San Diego and New York were taking their toll on all of us. So we moved his father to San Diego, where he could spend his remaining years in our loving care.

It was a difficult and tumultuous time for us. Reed put his life on hold for six years to take care of his father. It takes a rare human being to sacrifice that much of their life for someone else. Not too many people are willing to make the commitment to manage all the hospital visits, never-ending rotation of caregivers, and setting up of on-going hospice. It was a stressful learning experience. It's a miracle Reed and I survived all that life had thrown us and managed to stay together. But we did. Eventually, we got our happy ending living in Del Mar, California.

Fast forward to the year 2012. After twenty-three years in corporate America, I was stressed-out, burnt-out, exhausted, and feeling unappreciated. I wanted more for my life. It was time to decompress, unplug, and reevaluate life again.

My heart's desire was to create my own business, travel with Reed, and spend time with my aging parents. After experiencing Reed's father passing, it made me realize more than ever how precious my time with my parents was to me. I wanted to spend more quality time with them before it was too late. Momma was struggling with pulmonary fibrosis. Reed's father's death was a wake-up call for us to live our lives on our terms. So we downsized. We gave away a lot of stuff and packed away our remaining treasures in storage. We were ready for a break and an adventurous road trip.

We departed San Diego, California, on Feb. 15, 2013, to embark on a traveling adventure with our standard poodles, Ginger & Ambrose, in tow. It started with my soul-sister best friend Barbi's birthday celebration in Las Vegas. Then we spent time with my parents before we explored Lake Tahoe, Sun Valley Idaho, the Oregon coast, Washington and ultimately Vancouver Canada. It was just the traveling adventure we needed.

At some point during this journey, I reconnected with one of my amazing life coaches, Christopher. Once again the synchronicity of the angels was guiding me on my path. During one of our divinely guided strategy sessions, Christopher helped me tune into my soul gifts and a divine plan for creating my business and a life of happiness and success.

When we returned to San Diego the following year, in February 2014, we settled back in Del Mar with plans to re-launch our lives and businesses. A few weeks later, we were reminded that life is what happens when you're busy making plans. My brother George called with bad news. Poppa was in the emergency room with pneumonia and a blood infection. At

Introduction

86 years old, we were concerned, but Poppa wasn't. He had an amazing attitude that comforted us all in spite of his state of health. Three and a half weeks later, surrounded by his family, Poppa passed on to heaven.

Late in the evening of Poppa's memorial and life celebration, my sister and I had an intense discussion about life and relationships. Eventually, the stress of family pressures, taking care of Momma, and my own frustrations caused Reed and I to break up. We needed some distance, but my heart was in a quandary about the decision. We still loved each other very much.

Several weeks later, we planned to move out of our place in Del Mar we had moved into just a few months earlier. The move out weekend arrived. Our plans changed. We made a decision to reconcile our relationship. Reed stayed in Del Mar. I moved back to Las Vegas to care for my Momma. Poppa had been her primary caregiver prior to his passing.

After Poppa's passing, guided by a sixth sense, Reed called our friend Bob to talk about everything that had happened. Bob and his wife Danielle's pure love, support, and desire to teach and share from their life wisdom, revealed clarity, and provided a safe space for us to heal our hearts and get back together. We committed to the coaching and counseling support we needed to start over again. I followed my heart. The additional love, support, and understanding from my Momma and some of our closest friends helped us reunite and recommit to each other.

I was following in my parents' relationship footsteps. They were married for 20 years, then divorced. Ten years after they had divorced, they remarried and remained so for the last 25 years of their lives. When Momma announced she was remarrying my Poppa, during the weekend of my older brother George's wedding, I had many mixed emotions. It was strange how similar my relationship with Reed was to Momma's relationship with Poppa. She told me the story of how her Mom and several of her friends didn't want her to remarry Poppa. In spite of their opinions, Momma followed her heart instead of listening to them. Momma and Poppa loved each other very much. If they could make it against all odds so could Reed and I.

It was amazing grace that Momma joined Poppa in heaven within four months after he passed. She was surrounded by her family and an angelic hospice care team. I was blessed with parents who were my best friends. I'm grateful, at peace, and honored that I've experienced my life here on earth with them.

All the recent challenges of life had worn me down. I was sick and tired and feeling defeated by life. In spite of being sick, I forced myself to attend an event that empowered and inspired me about my future, even though I didn't realize it at the time. The only reason I went was I had invested $1,300 for my ticket and wasn't willing to throw that money away suffering at home sick.

After all that had transpired in my life, this is not how I thought life would turn out for me. My emotions were all over the place. As I gained clarity, I had to honor my own feelings and set up a new foundation for my life. Being sick weakened my resolve. I was feeling sad and sorry for myself. I felt worthless. Then I remembered the story of a guy who was down and out in his life. He had a coach who challenged him to live the next

Introduction

30-days as if they were his last. He said, "Okay," somewhat reluctantly, but realized he had nothing to lose. At the end of the thirty days, he had gained clarity and was filled with purpose. He understood why he was here. His story inspired me.

So why am I sharing the intimate details of my life story with you? Are you wondering what the point of all this is? Well, I'll tell you. In my journal, on March 26th, 2015 at 11:52 pm, I made a choice to live the next 30-days like they were my last. I committed to healing my broken heart and start taking care of me for a change, instead of everyone else.

I was ready to rediscover my passions in life. As I write this today, I realize I have embarked upon a miraculous journey. Gaining clarity about what my life purpose is has been healing for me. I feel blessed and grateful for who I am and for all that I've experienced. From the pure ecstasy of success, to the agony of defeat and betrayal, and everything in between, I have lived life fully. I've gained wisdom and understanding about who I am and what's important to me through my willingness to open my heart and understand myself better with the loving support of all the precious people in my life.

The triumph of success, pain of failure, and all the challenges I've endured forced me to grow into a better person. Through it all, my family and friends surround me in what I call a Circle of Love. I am eternally grateful for all that I've experienced, all of it. The good and the bad, the happy and the sad, have all molded me into the wise, successful, happy, resilient, courageous, passionate woman I am today.

My brother Todd has been with me every step of the way reminding me to "Go Big or Stay Home." That was his motto, which sparked the inspiration for mine. It's a slight variation, but one that makes a big difference. The motto I live by is ***Go Big AND Stay Home***. **At the core of *Go Big AND Stay Home* is the intention to honor your own hearts' desire and realize your dreams.** That's what this book is all about.

I did not realize I was actually going to write a book, until I met Ariela Wilcox, at the Women's Wisdom business networking lunch one day. Ariela is a one-of-a-kind Literary Agent who works with first time authors and business professionals. She's the only Literary Agent in the U.S. who oversees the writing of books. We met for a consultation. She intrigued me and got me thinking that maybe there was a book inside of me that needed to be written. I realized that I had a story to tell that might inspire others to, ***Go Big AND Stay Home***.

As a result of all my life experiences, I've learned to trust and honor my intuition. At our very first meeting, I knew Ariela was another earth angel who arrived in my life when I needed her. I was ready. She became my mentor and coach. There was a lot to do. The time was right for me to write my first book and rebrand my business, by leveraging my unique talents, gifts, and expertise, to monetize my wealth of knowledge. I was in good hands with Ariela's experience, guidance, and support to follow my heart to ***Go Big AND Stay Home***.

She inspired me to do what I do best. I seized the moment and set out on yet another amazing adventure to take my life to new heights. As the "#1 U.S. Leverage Expert", Ariela helped me see that I have a wealth of knowledge and resources that can help others soar to new heights in both their lives and businesses. Cheers to living life to the fullest and being grateful every breath of the way! The fun of creating something new began.

Introduction

Going for it and living life fearlessly makes me wiser, stronger, and more courageous everyday. My relationships with family, friends, and boyfriends have significantly influenced who I am. I see my relationships as miracles in my life. They continue to fascinate me with synchronicities and blessings.

As a result of my special gifts in nurturing and building relationships, I've become known as the Ambassador of Quality Connections and Strategic Alliances who helps people maximize connections and referrals. I inspire and motivate people to connect and grow a network of mutually supportive people who join forces to thrive and live life to the fullest.

The purpose for writing this book is to offer you secrets on how to connect with others and grow your network. I will share with you effective techniques for expanding your network and nurturing your relationships through referral partners, success circles, and harnessing the power of social networking. The courage to take risks and GO BIG starts with believing in yourself and being coachable. I've spent years accumulating and testing resources and systems to provide the support you need to soar to new heights in your life, business, and prosperity.

This book can help you if any of these questions hit home for you:

- Do you feel trapped or have you been hiding out in corporate America for your entire career?
- Are you nervous about your financial future?
- Do you secretly dream of having your own business, but are afraid to 'go for it?'
- Are you ready to try something new and perhaps take a little risk to discover and honor your life passions?

- Is now the time to start investing in 'you' to build your own business either part-time or full-time?

Be courageous. Take a leap of faith. Trust yourself. Invest in and nurture the precious relationships in your life. Like I do with my lifelong friend Julia. Our friendship started when we were babies and we've blossomed into trusted allies and confidants for each other. Also, Christopher who started as my business coach and now is an incredible business partner. My friend Barbi and I worked together on projects at Rare Medium. She became one of my best friends and we are both mutual fans of each other.

You will be pleasantly surprised at how a few things can be the catalyst to open doors to new opportunities to live the life of your dreams. Let me show you the way. I have resources, coaches, mentors, and invitations to amazing opportunities available at my fingertips to share with RAW individuals – people who are Ready, Able & Willing to live every day like it is their last.

Take action today. Get started. Let your presence be known. My forte is connecting you with the people and resources that have been the missing link for you until now. Take time to tune into "You" and dare to Live Your Dreams. The time is now. I invite you to join me on this exhilarating journey! Let's get started.

PART I:

FUNDAMENTALS FOR CONNECTING FACE-TO-FACE

Chapter 1:
Utilizing Success Circles,
Spiral Mapping & Master Mining

Go Big AND Stay Home will introduce you to the 21st Century model for doing business, by leveraging the power of technology while incorporating the art of building and nurturing relationships the old-fashioned way. I'll show you how to use the synergy of social networking, both in person and online, to grow your network exponentially. Using my fun and collaborative model, you'll be sure to significantly raise your income.

In this book, I reveal the required mindset and relationship building skills needed to create a solid foundation to launch a new business or revitalize your existing business. You'll learn how to supercharge your network connections and gain referrals that open up new opportunities for you to succeed and prosper.

After spending 23 years working in corporate America, I walked away from a six-figure income career because I was burnt out, stressed out, and unhappy. My mission was to unplug, decompress, travel, spend time with my aging parents and create my own business.

As a free spirit, I realized I was at a point in my life where I craved more freedom and appreciation than I was receiving in my corporate job. I dreamt of having a business that leveraged what I do naturally, networking and connecting people, to create win-win-win relationships. I help find the missing link that brings people together and seals the deal so everyone wins. The people I connect win, their clients win, and so do I. Here's a snapshot of my dream career and lifestyle.

**I have total freedom to live and
work anywhere in the world
doing what I love to do. I leverage my time by
connecting, referring, and empowering people
to prosper by expanding their networks.
My business makes money and
generates residual income
even while I'm sleeping.**

I achieve my dream career and lifestyle with the aide and support of other people. It is only possible with the right combination of resources.

I'll show you how to leverage the power of your relationships, so that you can invest your time, energy, and resources into your next big deal. I'll share with you a multi-faceted approach that includes resources, success tools, and access to experts who can guide, mentor, and coach you towards the success you dream of achieving.

By becoming a valuable resource to others you increase your worth and success. I'll show you how to grow your business and expand your network as a trusted resource. It starts with the spirit of giving. Think about how you can help and contribute to others, rather than what you can get from them. Give first. Help others get what they need and want first. Then they will be there when you need them. I am proof of that.

Have you ever had everything in your life change in an instant? I did when my brother died. I was devastated and heart-broken by the loss. I didn't know how I was going to get through life without him. My brother's death propelled me into a spiritual quest of self-discovery. Although his death was tragic and unwelcomed, I made sure good things came out of it. I had to make his death count for something. That quest has continued throughout my life.

Through the healing and loving support of the relationships in my life with teachers, counselors, coaches, friends, and family, I became who I am today.

Because of my desire and openness to learn, heal, and grow, I attract into my life the perfect people to support and guide me through whatever challenges I am encountering at any given time. I've experienced firsthand, "When the student is ready, the teacher will appear." I am infinitely grateful for all the teachers who appeared in my life when I needed them. I call them my 'earth angels'. They have filled many roles in my life as friends, mentors, teachers, and coaches.

My earth angel Coaches have helped me find my way through life. They empowered me to honor my passion and my truth, and create my life based on that foundation. They helped me actualize my dream of having my own business to achieve success and freedom on my terms. My coaches have saved me tons of time and money by helping me avoid costly mistakes. Having a coach is a fun and empowering way to streamline your efforts and take the fast track to success.

Successful Coaching is born out of a powerful partnership in which two minds strategize together to leverage your success. The effect and results are like magic. My coaching sessions with Christopher showed me how I could use my natural expertise for networking and connecting people with the power of a social media platform such as LinkedIn in my business. It was a recipe for success and a sound foundation on which to build my consulting business. I'll explain more about this in Chapter 4.

The relationships in my life are sacred. I feel fortunate and blessed. That's why I call my personal network my Circle of Love. That name originated from a party Reed and I hosted to celebrate our engagement and our love for each other with our family and friends. It was our special one-of-a-kind Circle of Love Celebration.

During one of my strategy sessions with Christopher, I visualized the sacred geometry of a spiral seashell. I saw myself in the center point of the spiral seashell. Fanning outwards from the center each layer represented the various layers of my relationships. This was the inspiration from which I created the process called **Spiral Mapping** and **Master Mining** your network.

One day while I was walking on the beach I found several beautiful seashells. Most days of the week, I walk on the beach barefoot to get rejuvenated and connect with mother earth. I enjoy spending time picking up seashells and colorful rocks on the beach. Sand dollars and spiral shells are two of my favorite gifts from the sea. I'm amazed at their intricate details and in awe of their journey to arrive on the beach near my home. Finding these treasures of the sea are like experiencing little miracles that make up some of the simplest pleasures in my life.

While reflecting upon the simple beauty of a seashell, I made a correlation between seashells and the magic of networking relationships. Relationships and connections are like seashells in that there is an evolution and mystery on how one person can have a huge impact and make such a simple and yet significant difference in the lives of those they touch and connect with.

Next time you see a seashell check out its sacred geometry. Notice how it fans out from the center point so eloquently. I am at the nexus, center of the sacred geometry of my relationships and they fan out around me. Each of us are connected and impact each other in a myriad of ways. Who are the people closest to you in your life? Who knows your heart best? Have you ever thought about this, or do you take them all for granted? Have you ever made a list of your core "go-to" relationships?

Relationships are about the **Quality** of connections versus **Quantity**. For example, if highly connected people like Tony Robbins, Oprah Winfrey, Richard Branson, Deepak Chopra, Madonna, and Panache Desai were in my Circle of Love, I would have access to the world via my network! I would have a very powerful network with less than one hundred people in it, because of the quality of people in it. Who are the people in your world giving you access to the universe? Eliminate the people who are taking up space and sucking air from your dreams. Let them go with grace, to make room for people who are a better fit for you and what you're up to in life.

Build and grow your network so that everyone is synergistically connected, aligned, and harmonized with each other.

What is *Spiral Mapping* and *Master Mining* your network and how does it work? One day, I focused on my contacts and all the people in my network. I had over 2,000 names in my database when I resigned from my nine-year career of marketing and business development at Heritage Escrow. This seemed like a lot of contacts to me at the time. I hadn't discovered the power of social media yet. This was a real list of people I knew and had met or done business with over the years. Instead of suffering the tedious task of searching through every single name on that list of 2,000 people, I allowed my intuition to lead me through an organic process I developed called Spiral Mapping and Master Mining Your Network to segregate the list into my three core Success Circles: A, B, C. As I organized the list, I started to see the power and potential of how I could leverage it. It was exciting.

**Methodology for Spiral Mapping and
Master Mining A, B, C Success Circles.
*Reference Spiral Seashell Illustration:**

- Schedule 20-minutes a day over the course of a week to go through the process of organizing your list into your core Success Circles.
- Create memory triggers by thinking about all the jobs you've had and all the key people in your network, like your mentors, coaches, leaders, and coworkers from every company you've worked for.
- Write down names on a piece of paper or create a list in a spreadsheet in your computer. You can even create a list on your mobile phone in the Notes section.
- Keep a running list of these names and continue adding to your list.
- Copy/type the names into a spreadsheet. Label each person A, B, or C and sort the list. Save the document.
- Your "A Team" consists of people who are your confidants, mentors, and coaches. They are people

you influence and who influence you. These people are your inner circle.

- Your "B Team" consists of important people too, but they are your second tier people. They are the second circle out on the spiral, as shown in the spiral illustration. These are the people you rely on when your A Team people aren't available.
- Your "C Team" is the third section of the spiral. It's comprised of people you have heard of via your A and B Teams. They may be referrals from the people closest to you that you may want to meet. A "C Team" person may also be someone you met at a networking event, felt a kindred spirit connection with, and/or have a business opportunity to share with them.

Label your A, B, C Success Circle teams in the way that makes the most sense for you. It depends on your business and how your mind works. The key to successfully leverage your network is to know it well and have it easily accessible for quick reference. This has been the key to my success and will be the key to yours too if you use it. This is a simple but effective process.

Recently, I was reminded of the power of having my A, B, C Success Circle list available. A close friend of mine, Manna, who was working on a Real Estate Investment Trust Project (REIT), asked if I had any resources in my network that would be interested in investing in the REIT, or becoming partners in the project. Almost immediately a few people came to mind that could be good contacts for her. Then when I referenced my A, B, C Success Circle list, I realized I had forgotten a particular person who could be a key contact for her. Having my own reference library of resources available at my fingertips made me realize how important a business asset my list of contacts was, not only for me, but for my friend and the rest of my network too.

If I hadn't had that list it would have been a missed opportunity to help someone in my network. That list increased my value to her. Creating, growing, and organizing a strong list of contacts that is accessible at all times is one of the most powerful assets you can use to grow your business. Want to become invaluable to your network? Use your list to be the "go-to" person who helps people in your network.

Having a list isn't enough. It's the quality of that list that matters. You need to analyze your list to discover its true value. For example, I realized that out of the 2,000 people in my database, only 110 of them were in my core A, B, and C Success Circles. Analyzing the list got me in touch with the reality of the numbers. Only 5% of the people in my database were on my "go-to" team.

When you evaluate the contacts in your network, don't get discouraged if you discover that you only have 10 people or less in your core Success Circles. It takes time to build a quality list of contacts, but it pays off when you see the possibilities of growing that list to hundreds, maybe even thousands or millions through social media channels. You've got to start somewhere. Can you see how important it is to nurture those relationships in your life? It may pay off for you or someone you know one day.

Going through this process reminded me of the importance of those people closest to me and why nurturing those relationships is so powerful. By tending to the garden of my life, my relationships, it became clear to me how one person can be the seed that can grow into something beautiful that makes a huge difference in my life. It's exciting for me to witness the power of this realization in my clients too.

When I was considering leaving the construction industry and going into Sales, my first thought was, who in my network is in sales that could help me connect to new opportunities in sales? There were so many options to pursue and consider. Is their company hiring? Do they know of a company that is hiring? Would they refer me as a potential candidate to their contact at that company? It is much easier to get your foot in the door of big companies through a referral. Even big companies would much rather hire someone that is referred rather than a complete stranger.

Relationships are my stealth resource. They can be yours too if you are willing to connect and invest time in getting to know the people in your network by asking questions to learn more about them, their business, history, and network of connections.

I was networking with my friend Suzanne one day. She was super successful in sales. During our conversation she referred me to someone she thought could help me. As a result of following up on that referral, it helped me make a smooth transition into my new career in sales.

My networking efforts helped me strategically make a career transition from the construction industry into sales that increased my income by 30%. Although I was ready for something new, I am forever grateful for all that I learned and everyone I met in my Construction Engineering career. Many of those people are still in my network today. Working with Taylor Woodrow, on the John Wayne Airport project in Irvine California, and for the Walt Disney Company, laid a solid foundation and instilled in me a strong work ethic that has helped me achieve the level of success I have in my sales, marketing, and business development career.

It was shortly after I started my new career in sales at Kodak that my brother Todd was killed. Even though I was devastated, starting out on a new career path in sales actually helped me cope with the loss as I threw myself into my new career. It helped me survive the grief.

The power of relationships saved me again. There was a guy at work, Stephen, who left a sympathy card on my desk. I was surprised and touched by this random act of kindness by someone I barely knew. Needless to say, Stephen and I became great friends. Even though Stephen eventually left Kodak to pursue other opportunities, we stayed in touch. That was the start of yet another lasting and loving friendship that continues to enrich my life today. We enjoy lots of laughter and fun every time we get together.

A year after Stephen left Kodak he recruited me for a hot opportunity. He was the Vice President of Sales at a new Internet company called RareMedium.com. I remember thinking at the time, *how am I going to work for an Internet company when I barely know how to use email?* I was not a technology wiz to say the least. But through the power of my network, knowing Stephen opened the door and invited me into a whole new fascinating world of technology that I continue to master today. Thank you, Stephen, for thinking of me and believing in me until I could believe in myself!

My friendship with Stephen opened the door to a new career path for me, but it was my past career that helped me learn how to succeed in my new one. I had an epiphany one day while prepping for my interview. I realized that building a website was like constructing a building. I was able to use my experience and expertise from a previous career and apply it to my new one.

I learned that, like a building, a website starts with an idea/concept that is brought to life by the collaboration of a team. Next, the project budget and timeline are created for all aspects of the project. The project foundation, technical back-end of a website, is built in order for a website to function, just as a building's foundation is engineered and built to support the structure of the building. What the majority of people see are the creative results of a completed project. The technical and engineering aspects of the foundations are rarely seen, unless you were part of the team who built the project. I was hired for my fearless nature and ability to build, create, and nurture relationships, in order to sell our turnkey web development services.

Referrals are more effective than cold calls because the person referring you already knows your skills so they can recommend you with confidence. They open the door for you to develop a new relationship.

This new career catapulted me into a new stratosphere of financial success. I was thrilled. My income doubled. I was proud to be part of the history of the birth of the Internet and websites. It was a whirlwind of excitement and learning back then. Business was moving so fast and so was I. I learned more about business in those two years than most people learn in their lifetime.

The company grew daily from a penny stock to over $100 per share. Many of us were millionaires on paper. It was an exhilarating time in my life to be a part of the action, until it suddenly crashed and burned. During the stock market frenzy and the burst of the dot-com bubble, our stock price plummeted. Fortunately, I continued to expand my network so I had an escape route. I met Stephen's sister Connie when she was visiting from San Diego. I didn't realize it at the time just how valuable and serendipitous that meeting would turn out to be for me later.

Eventually, I left Los Angeles and moved to San Diego. Stephen and I stayed in touch. He suggested I call his sister to find out if the company she was working for was hiring. He said, "Tracie, you would be a perfect fit. You get paid to build relationships, and wine and dine clients." Connie was my "in" for the first interview. I was hired to start yet another career transition into a completely new industry at Heritage Escrow.

Here's an example of the power of networking. People were not hired in the escrow business unless they were already in the residential real estate industry and locals who had lived in the area long enough to know it well. Because of my friendship with Connie, I landed an interview with the Sales Manager. That led to an interview with the Vice President of Sales and I was hired! Because I knew someone on their team, and I had sales skills, they agreed to take a chance on me.

While I worked at Heritage Escrow, I created strategic alliances with title representatives and mortgage lenders in my geographic area. I created a Success Circle of power partners that enabled us to do things together that none of us could have achieved individually. We hosted events with top speakers and created exclusive weekly pitch sessions for realtors in Rancho Santa Fe and Del Mar. We referred business to each other, because of our strategic alliance and business synergy together.

Word got out. I had earned a great reputation. The referrals started flowing in. My team was closing escrows left and right, even though those real estate agents had been loyal to other escrow companies for years. They hired my team because they appreciated my efforts and were willing to give us a chance to win over their business. And we did! It was a salesperson's dream. New clients called to say, "Thank you, for all you do in the community to support our business." It was such a fun and rewarding way to do business for all of us!

Open up new opportunities to succeed and prosper by Master Mining Your Network. Ask yourself:
- How am I forming referral partners?
- Who do I have strategic alliances with?
- Am I creating Success Circles for lead generation to build my sales pipelines?
- Am I scheduling time to meet with the core people in my network to build synergistic partnerships where everybody wins?

Dig for the gold in your network through your relationships. You never know just how close you are to making a golden connection that could be the catalyst for starting a new career that doubles your income. Be consistent, systematic, and strategic, in how you nurture and develop the relationships in your network. You never know who could be the next link that increases your odds of striking gold. I have so many success stories to share about how who you know gets you where you want to go.

David Michail's Story

David started his legal career in Southern California because of a referral from a relationship he had. Since 1998, David has had an exciting career as an attorney on the forefront of technology, media, and the entertainment industry. He advises Fortune 500 companies and companies in emerging markets on how to protect their intellectual property while doing business via the Internet and social media. Here's what David has to say about the power of networking:

"After serving as Chief Operating Officer and General Counsel for two Virginia companies by the age of 23, I thought I had enough experience under my belt to get a decent job in Los Angeles. I was wrong. I had no contacts except for a few people who knew my girlfriend, Danielle, who eventually became my wife.

It was during 1999 when the dot-com economy offered a myriad of opportunities for a young energetic attorney like me. However, no one knew who I was or what I was capable of doing. I didn't have a competitive advantage, coming from a rural area in Virginia, as I tried to connect in a big city like Los Angeles.

Employers weren't impressed by my East Coast law school expertise. They didn't care about my triumphs as a young C.O.O. and General Counsel. It was at that young age that I discovered the hard truth about building networks, alliances, and obligations to amplify my career. I started from ground zero. It wasn't pretty. I worked during the day as a personal trainer, and in the evenings as a lawyer taking on small matters for my wife's friends to make ends meet and cover the rent.

One day, Tracie Hasse, a close friend of my wife Danielle, told me that Rare Medium, a web services company she was working for, was hiring. She helped me get an interview in their venture capital department.

I had never worked for a venture capital firm before. I didn't have any experience in that area. I had done some legal work for a small investment banking company as a result of a referral from one of my girlfriend's connections. Tracie thought that experience was relevant enough and encouraged me to go for it. She thought I would be a great fit at Rare Medium. I don't think my soon-to-be-boss was that impressed with me at first. I think it was Tracie's persistence and his immediate need to get an attorney in there to put deals together that got me my first attorney job in LA.

Once I was in, I was able to win him over and prove my abilities to navigate the rough waters of big corporate transactions. I survived there for about a year after the dot-com bubble burst. Then Rare Medium had to close its operations in Los Angeles. It was time to either find another job or start up my own law practice. Naively, I chose to go for it on my own. That made more sense to me at the time, because the market was flooded with unemployed corporate Internet attorneys looking for work after the dot-com bubble burst.

Fortunately, I learned how to network while at Rare Medium. I had built a reputation for getting deals done. So when the talent from Rare Medium dispersed and reconfigured themselves into small creative agencies throughout the country, they all called me to help them get their new businesses started.

Sixteen years and hundreds of clients later, I've been able to build my own successful legal practice because of the global network I have developed. It's a good thing I didn't know initially how hard it would be to start my own business. There were many months of struggling to make ends meet. I learned by trial and error how to build a strong network of quality professionals I could count on to bring value to my business. Learning how to network has become an invaluable skill that enabled me to launch my career as an attorney in Southern California. I am grateful that Tracie believed in me enough to refer me to that opportunity at Rare Medium, and that I seized the moment and went for it."

David's story illustrates the benefits of how Master Mining works. Master Mining Your Network has huge benefits and pay offs if you learn to do it well.

Success Circles were created out of Spiral Mapping and Master Mining. Whether I am looking for a job, building referral pipelines, or looking to start a new business, the people I go to are my A, B, and C, Success Circles. This is an organic process and ever evolving. It requires maintenance, as some relationships deepen and prevail while others serve their purpose and move on.

**The best part about Success Circles
is that there is no hierarchy**.

Napoleon Hill's timeless book, *Think and Grow Rich*, was written in 1937 and is still a popular book about success today. Groups of people gather weekly or monthly in small groups to study the principles in that book in order to learn how to achieve greater success and wealth. I consider those groups Success Circles. Some of my friends have even formed *Think and Grow Rich* study groups to learn how to apply the principles of success and wealth in their lives.

Success Circles can help you build your list of A, B, and C connections with a group of like-minded people who are committed to getting together regularly for camaraderie and resource sharing. Have fun creating your own Success Circles for your personal and business life.

Build Community One Success Circle at a Time

Success Circles are cooperative, collaborative communities of like-minded people who connect to support each other by referring resources that help everyone grow professionally and personally.

How to Set-Up a Success Circle:

1. **Call to connect**: Make a personal phone call first, and follow-up with text or email.

2. **Schedule appointment:** Keep the call brief, 30 seconds or less. You're on a mission. Leave a message if they aren't there. Suggest a couple of meeting times for them to choose from.

3. **Find a Meeting Location:** Find a location that is suitable for the size of your group and provides the privacy and conditions needed to share resources with each other.

4. **Meet and Greet**: At the meeting learn about each other, your businesses, and how you can all become a strong referral network for each other. Determine the structure and expectations for the group.

5. **Expand the Circle**: Look for Power Partners to invite to join your Success Circle. Who else do each of you have in common that would be a good fit for your Success Circle?

6. **Social Media**: Connect on LinkedIn and Facebook to leverage your relationships with each other. See how you're connected.

7. **Grow and Prosper**: Continue to invite guests and Power Partners to grow your Success Circle into a community of referral resources.

For example, start by choosing three to five friends who want to change their life by learning how to create more revenue in addition to their full time job. The premise of the Success Circle is to support each other in the attainment of mutual goals by contributing valuable information and resources to each other. Schedule the group to meet in person either weekly, biweekly or monthly, whatever works best for everyone in the group. You could even have virtual meetings and use online resources to connect.

Over 15 years ago, my friends and I created *SpaCap Ladies* Success Circle. We thought it would be a fun way to stay connected. The premise was to learn about the stock market, educate each other, and invest in stocks selected by the group. We started out meeting in Newport Beach. Then over the years, work opportunities and family obligations scattered everyone across the states. So we scheduled monthly conference calls. We had action items for our call that kept us learning and moving forward.

Each year we all met up at a resort for a reunion to spend our investment wins pampering ourselves with a Spa experience. This was a fun Success Circle that kept our friendships going strong. To this day, we are all still connected and minding our own investments.

The relationships you create in Success Circles are through an organic process. When a Success Circle's goal is achieved, that particular group may fade away because it has fulfilled its purpose. Or perhaps, when a goal is achieved another one is created so the Success Circle continues. You can be involved in many Success Circles that serve different purposes in your life personally and professionally. One of the many rewards of Success Circles is the deep and lasting friendships that are cultivated between members.

So many times in life we give up on our dreams for different reasons, often other people and outside influences cause us to doubt ourselves and our dreams. Maybe someone told you that you were a failure so why even try. Did you know that Thomas Edison, the inventor of the light bulb, found 9,999 ways that a light bulb didn't work, before he found on his 10,000th attempt the one way that it did work? The rest is history.

Most people wouldn't even try something nine or 10 times, let alone 10,000. How about you? What was it that kept Thomas Edison moving forward until he succeeded? He saw opportunities where others saw failure. He interpreted perceived failures as temporary setbacks, not failure. You can't fail if you don't give up. Failure is giving up before you've achieved your goal. It was his mindset and faith in what he believed possible that kept him moving forward to realize his dream, in spite of others perceiving him as a failure.

I've had my share of failures, as well as many successes. During a call with my life coach, Bob, I had an epiphany when recalling my time as a gymnast. I started gymnastics at the age of ten. During my first few years I thrived and won many awards in competitions that culminated in winning the 1976 Nevada State

All-Around Champion Gymnast award. What an honor it was to win this award. My dedication and commitment to my practice paid off.

Shortly after that exciting success, I started getting injured. I found myself in a terrible cycle of getting better, then getting injured again. I pushed through, because as an athlete that is what I was trained to do. Two years later I had to quit gymnastics because of my injuries. I felt like a failure because I didn't excel in that sport any longer. It was a crushing blow to my ego to leave the sport under these conditions.

Then I tried out for the cheerleading team in junior high and succeeded in making the team two years in a row. Then during my junior year I had a blow to my ego when I lost the cheerleading competition and didn't make the junior team. In my senior year, I made a comeback when I succeeded in the competition and made the songleading dance team. That was even more fun because it combined cheerleading and dancing. I was having the time of my life performing at the high school assemblies and football and basketball games.

Reflecting on my experiences with my life coach helped me see a pattern of how I dealt with great success then dismal failures in my career and life. I considered myself a failure when I tried to build many independent businesses in various industries from legal help to skincare without much success. Those failures were compounded by a string of failed romantic relationships. I never wanted to feel the pain of defeat and my ego kept me in denial as I refused to acknowledge these failures. I covered these feelings up by focusing on my next success. Then I would succeed and start making money again and forget about the failures.

Bob suggested that instead of resisting these memories I should revisit them. He helped me understand the impact those feelings of failure from the past were having on me in the present. He helped me see that they had never really gone away. I had never dealt with those feelings so they were still trapped inside of me and affecting my life decades later. I had resisted them instead of feeling them. Did you know that what you resist persists? My ego did everything to bury those feelings deep inside, yet those feelings of failure were still there, no matter how much my ego tried to convince me otherwise.

I've learned that by acknowledging my ego, I can consciously give myself permission to feel all my feelings, the feelings of success as well as the feelings of failure. Rather than thinking of myself as a failure, I chalk it up to learning lessons from a life experience. Now I am proud of myself for at least having the courage to take a risk and try something new. Understanding, accepting, and allowing myself to actually feel my feelings when I experience setbacks and failures has enriched me as a person and enabled me to learn from all the experiences in my life, the failures as well as the successes.

**Life is a phenomenal adventure of freedom
when you give yourself permission
to be your authentic self.**

By accepting the ups and downs of life, it has helped me establish a deeper faith and trust in myself and my ability to survive, thrive, and succeed. I've learned to let go of trying so hard to force outcomes and started trusting the power of just being. I live life deliberately, aware, relaxed, breathing, trusting, and tuning in to all of me now.

Barbi's Story:

It only takes one person in your network to shift everything for you from striving and struggling to flowing and prospering doing what you love. You never know who that person is going to be, and typically it's someone you least expect. I asked my soul-sister best friend Barbi, how she went from struggling and trying so hard to make things happen to be noticed and seen in her business, to thriving as an event planner and designer who creates outrageous, experiential events internationally through her company *Considerate Done* with grace, brilliance, and joy.

This is what she said:

"I had started my event design and production business, Considerate Done, and was working diligently to grow it. As you know, clients are the number one goal for a growing business. My approach, the thing that had always worked for me, was to push as hard as possible until things finally fell into place, kind of like pushing a huge boulder up hill. So I proceeded as usual. I talked to everyone I knew and took any and every project that came my way, no matter how big or small.

I had forgotten my sales 101 skills regarding qualifying clients and opportunities to determine if they were indeed what I was looking for and a good fit. I was mired in the depths of pushing. I exhausted myself with endless "creative projects" to demonstrate my talent and skills. I engaged in both personal and "free of charge" ventures for friends and family. I was trapped in a vicious cycle, like a hamster running a marathon on a wheel that was going nowhere. The truth of the situation was I was really not making any gains. I was still relying on my consulting skills in the web services space to earn an income. For many years, I earned very little in my dream business as a creative event designer. That's why the events that led up to landing my largest corporate client were quite serendipitous.

In my spare time, I was working in our yard, feeding my desire to create beauty and build something. I became friends with an older retired couple across the street. They were always outside working on their garden too, so we decided it might be fun to work together on our various projects. It was great to have the company and to learn about gardening and life as we spent hours together beautifying our southern California postage stamp lots.

One day during one of our conversations, they asked if I had met their neighbor, the one living beside them. They thought we would really hit it off. Soon we had a new neighbor, Sally, join our gardening sessions and a friendship began to blossom.

Sally and I became close friends quickly. We had a lot in common. In addition to gardening, the fact that we were both Southern Girls deepened our bond as we enjoyed many adventures together. The greatest adventure and grandest bonding experience took place when she approached me to assist in planning her daughter's wedding. She was terribly upset one day and through our conversation I discovered it was about her daughter's wedding. So many details had not been attended to and addressed. All she could see was a train wreck in the making, basically a nightmare unwinding.

The wedding date was approaching quickly and there was still so much that was not done. So we joined forces and made a fierce team as we tackled all that needed to get done considering the short timeline. We worked together day and night, flew to Houston and back several times, and finally landed in Austin to bring it all home. The wedding was gorgeous and more beautiful than expected. One of Sally's worst nightmares had been averted and our friendship had grown even stronger. I was glad I was there to help a friend during a stressful time and that it turned out to be such a success. This was another "free of charge" friend and family project that I had done.

Many years later, her husband was having a conversation with her about entertaining clients for his business. He was running ideas by her. During their conversation, Sally recalled all she and I had done to pull off their daughter's wedding. She realized that my skill set would be perfect for this opportunity. She recommended her husband call me to discuss the possibility of working together. I created a proposal and pitched my ideas for a corporate event he was hosting in Chicago. He liked my creative concepts so much that he awarded me the business and I got paid for it! One party turned into two and then four and now 11 years later I am producing ten global events every year for him. He has become my largest client.

So what does all of this mean? Why does it matter? Through this experience I learned a very valuable lesson. Things that are meant to be do not need to be "pushed" into existence. When something is meant for you it will find you and its success is inevitable. My years of efforting and giving so much of myself away in hopes of landing clients had proven futile. As I contemplated this, I realized I lacked discernment early on and said yes to every opportunity hoping it would eventually become a viable income producing connection. The truth was that none of the "efforting" opportunities materialized into anything real for my business.

I was highly motivated to change my approach after witnessing how easy it was to attract my best client. I simply harnessed the power of a friendship, which led me to effortless success and happiness doing what I love to do and getting paid well to do it.

Now I have a much greater level of discernment regarding opportunities and people that are a good fit for my services. I have an actual gut feeling for what is right and good. The indication of this is that it feels good and moves forward without pushing. So, in a nutshell, my advice is always, always, always trust your internal compass which is that gut feeling so many talk about. It will never fail you. Honor the power of your relationships. Let your friends know what you love to do and show them. Ask them to keep you in mind for opportunities to do what you love to do. Trust that it will happen when it's meant to be."

This is just one of the many inspiring stories of people who experienced the benefits of someone in their network referring them to an opportunity that changed their lives for the better.

This book is an invitation to join me on this journey, in the hopes that it will inspire you to take advantage of the wealth of resources you already have surrounding you in your own network of personal and professional relationships.

My intention is to be a resource to help you build a strong network you can count on. I've included inspirational stories, nuggets of wisdom, and business insights from decades of business experience to help you on your journey of Master Mining Your Network. All of this is to help you succeed and prosper with ease through the power of effective networking.

Ch. 1 Recap: Proactive Prosperity

Thought Provoking Questions to Think About

- Do you aspire to *Go Big AND Stay Home*? What does that mean for you?
- How can you create your own Success Circles within your personal and business networks?
- Look in your own life at how a relationship or connection has helped you make an important connection or transition in your career or life.
- How could you have more success in your life and business by tapping into the power of referrals from your network?
- What's the first step you can take this week to expand your network and develop powerful referral partnerships?

Mindful Reflections

- Referrals are powerful because the person referring you knows you and your skills so they can recommend you with confidence.
- Create Success Circles through Spiral Mapping and Mastering Mining Your Network.
- Life is a phenomenal adventure of freedom when you give yourself permission to be your authentic self.
- Write down your dream career and lifestyle. Don't try to figure out how it's all going to happen. Have fun with it.

PART II:
THE POWER OF CONNECTING ONLINE

Chapter 2:
Connecting Online & Offline
with Purpose & Intention

Be the resource your network can't live without! When you connect your clients to resources that help them get what they want or need, everyone benefits from the connections you make. As the catalyst, you create synergistic partnerships that generates income for all involved.

Are you the "go-to" person your network calls on to find and fill in the missing pieces to their jigsaw puzzle? It may be a person, service, product, or an idea that you provide that helps them. Once you help them find that missing link, you become invaluable to them because you've helped them complete their puzzle and get unstuck.

Your job is to lead the way in your network by referring business to others first without being concerned about whether or not they will reciprocate. Be the person who takes the lead to schedule a meeting with your potential referral partners to discuss how you can help each other grow your businesses through referrals. Be prepared to follow through when others refer business to you.

Discuss the terms of referrals. Do you want to pay each other a referral fee? Consider either a flat rate fee or a percentage like a 10% referral fee paid for the initial client consult, or on the initial project. This is a fun way to do business because everyone wins. Have conversations with people in your network to set up referral agreements that allow you to prosper from having connected resources.

Create a Referral Agreement that you both sign and honor as a business contract. It can be a simple one-page agreement or a formal legal contract. Make sure your Referral Agreement includes these bare minimum requirements:

1. Date

2. Names of Referral Partners

3. Description of Business

4. What the referrals are for

5. The referral fee amount agreed upon to pay each other

6. Timing of payment

7. Confirmation/signature line.

LegalShield, noted in the Resources section, or a business attorney can write up a formal referral contract for you.

One of my favorite things to do is send a referral check with a handwritten Thank You note to the person who referred business to me. It's a nice personal touch. It's rare to receive a hand written Thank You in the mail these days. Most of us rely on emails. But, when you take a little extra time and effort to do something more personal you get people's attention and stand out. They appreciate the more personal touch and extra effort.

If I could sum up what my life theme has been in a phrase, it would be *Relationship Marketing*. When I'm in need of a specific resource, I have mastered the art of going to my network of relationships by tapping into my Success Circles to find the resource I need. I've learned from decades of experience to trust that my network of relationships has what I need.

The mindset of Success Circles is to give without expecting to get. Think about how you can help others first. Then they will help you too.

There may be times, when what is great for you, may not be great for another. At my 30th birthday celebration, 30 of my closest friends orchestrated a weekend birthday party at Catalina Island. It was one of the best birthday parties ever. I had a total blast. I saw the beauty and the best in each one of my guy friends and girlfriends. What I was not expecting was for any of my friends not to like each other. Wow was I in for a surprise as I heard from several of my friends, "Why do you like him? He's such a jerk" or "She's such a witch." I learned a lot about people that weekend. Just because I like someone does not mean someone else will like him or her too.

I've learned to live and let live, and see the beauty in people. We all have lessons to learn and challenges to overcome. We all have a unique purpose for being here. Just because someone is different doesn't mean that you shouldn't accept him or her for being who they are.

The same principle applies to business. There will be people you like and others you don't click with. That's okay, but how you handle it could impact you more than you know. There may be times when a referral does not work out for the person you referred them to. That is part of the process. Some people are meant to do business with each other and others aren't. You will never know unless you try.

Connecting online AND in-person is like oxygen and water to the body. You cannot live without one or the other. Both are critical to your survival. There are a multitude of options for connecting with people to grow your network of contacts and thrive in business. Today people are connecting in ways ranging from face-to-face at networking events, casually with family and friends, and online via the social media channels. Don't do just one or the other, do both face-to-face and online networking. Otherwise, you will miss out on opportunities. I challenge you to expand beyond your comfort zone.

11 Benefits of Connecting Face-to-Face

1. **Builds rapport:** It's easier to build rapport with someone in-person than it is online.

2. **It is fun and social:** It creates a friendly atmosphere of camaraderie as you discover new places when meeting people.

3. **Like attracts like**: You can tune into other people's energy and get a better sense of who they are and observe how you feel around them.

4. **Quality Connections**: Face-to-Face meetings have a more personal touch that can energize your network with new clients and unexpected resources.

5. **Top of mind**: Out of sight, out of mind. Be in front of people so they remember you are available to help them. Invite your friends to join in the fun to make connections too.

6. **Leaves a Lasting Impression**: It's easier to leave a lasting impression in person than online because you can leverage your peers to make introductions.

7. **Lead Conversion**: In person you have the advantage of reading facial expressions and body gestures in order to adjust your approach to convert prospects into new clients.

8. **Eye-to-Eye Contact**: You can look them in the eye, shake hands, and connect physically to build a warmer relationship in-person than online.

9. **Celebrate victories together**: All work and no play makes an entrepreneur a dull business owner. A network that celebrates successes together grows and stays together.

10. **Appreciation**: You get to work your magic by acknowledging and appreciating others in person, which fuels the fire of your connection.

11. **Community**: Connecting with people in-person reminds you that you're not alone. You have physical proof that you are part of a community of friends who support you.

Once you've made your initial connection with someone face-to-face, leverage technology to stay connected.

11 Reasons to Connect Online and Get Linked

1. **Word of mouth** expands exponentially to **world of mouth**

2. **Maximizes opportunities** efficiently

3. **Expands your reach** to market yourself

4. **Increases your exposure** so others can find you more easily

5. **Enhances your communication and marketing efforts**

6. **Discover New Connections** with a quick visual reference of your contacts that's easily accessible online so you can leverage the connections of your network.

7. **Go Viral**: New ideas travel faster than the speed of a click, which could cause a sudden surge of success in your business.

8. **Cost effective**: Most social media channels are FREE.

9. **Leverage technology** to automate your networking and marketing efforts.

10. **Grow your network while you sleep**: Social media provides a global network of people who can connect with you 24-hours a day, even while you sleep.

11. **Just do it**: Start growing your network. Go Online today!

Can you see the power of doing both and how they mutually enhance your networking efforts? Meet face-to-face and then get linked online to stay connected.

Do you ever wonder why people pick 3 tips, 7 secrets, or 11 reasons when writing an article or a book? I'm a numbers person. I'm intrigued by Numerology. I tend to notice the clock when it is 11:11 or combinations of numbers that are Birthdays of my loved ones. Years ago I started making wishes when I'd see 11:11 on a clock or there was an auspicious date on the calendar like 11/11/11. From my understanding it is a time when you have extra heaven and earth luck on your side. I found this very fun, and thought some extra good luck sounds like a winner to me. Every time I see 11:11, I make a wish in that moment.

When my fiancé Reed and I got engaged, people asked us, "When is the wedding?" We didn't know. We hadn't picked a date yet. Before my parents and his dad made their transitions to heaven we wanted to have some kind of celebration while they were still here on planet earth. I had an epiphany in the middle of the night. Let's have a Circle of Love Celebration on

November 11th (11/11) to celebrate our love, and our love for our family and friends, and send it out to the world! I looked at the calendar in the middle of the night and could have sworn 11/11 landed on a Saturday that year.

It was September and we had just moved into a home in the hills of Del Mar, a magical place where we both wanted to live. Our mission for our Circle of Love celebration was to find a home on the beach in Del Mar for our guests to experience a taste of our life and all the things we loved and celebrated with our favorite foods and colorful flowers, music, and each other. After exhausting all my resources in real estate to secure an oceanfront property to rent for a three-day weekend, it seemed like trying to find a needle in a haystack. I had one remaining property left on my list to check out.

One day during the weekly Del Mar Realtor pitch session I conducted, the last person to speak up was Marcia. She shared information about her beachfront rental property. I could not believe it. She was the realtor responsible for the last property on my list. Reed and I met up with her the next day, shared our love story and desire to kick off the party on 11/11, and the significance of that date for us. It was exactly one month prior to 11/11 when we met with Marcia. She shared how both her and her father loved when they saw 11:11 too. The owner of the property typically rented out that beach property for a week minimum, but was willing to rent it to us for our three-day weekend with nearly 100 guests of family and friends, to celebrate our Circle of Love!

It was a party like no other as we introduced our family and friends to sound healing, enjoyed delicious food from our favorite restaurants and the beauty of Del Mar, while celebrating our commitment ceremony on the beach surrounded in a circle by our loved ones, with the spectacular San Diego weather and beautiful sunset to top it off.

I share this story because it is so meaningful on many levels. Most importantly, we had a vision and put our intention out to the universe. We took action and did our part in planning and connecting with the people we love to bring the celebration to fruition. We almost gave up but hung in there. We mapped out our timeline and what had to happen along the way in order to put on our event. One of the items on the list was to secure a property one month in advance. If we were not successful in securing the place, we felt it was not meant to be. We kept the faith and felt in our heart and soul that this party was meant to be.

I remember thinking earlier in the day before I met Marcia that maybe this party might not happen. I was bummed at that possibility, but I was willing to accept it. I gave this possibility a place to be rather than resisting it. I knew I had one more contact to make, and if it did not work out, I felt it was not meant to be in the way and time I thought it would be. Then Marcia came to the rescue and the story had a happy ending. It was such a magical celebration that we are grateful for and will never forget!

The domino effect of creating and nurturing yourself and great relationships brings to mind a recent experience I had with a new friend, Marina. I met Marina at a networking party I was invited to attend. I was going to the event to make introductions to connect people I thought would have some business synergy with each other. At this event, Marina won a raffle prize for another networking event hosted by the same group a few weeks later.

I followed up with Marina after that event. During that call she realized she needed my consulting services. She hired me and we had our first LinkedIn strategy session two days later. She invited me to the networking event she had won the raffle prize for. And I invited her to a group I was a member of, Women's Wisdom that I thought she could benefit from the following week. Marina seized the opportunity and met me at Women's Wisdom.

Women's Wisdom is a business networking group that was established in 1991 by Judy Ann Foster, to empower women in friendship and business, by providing monthly networking events with dynamic speakers and a forum to learn, connect, receive, and create business synergies. Women's Wisdom is more than a networking event. It is a community of some of the top women business leaders in the country who are making a difference in the world. If you are ever in San Diego, I encourage you to check it out.

As a result of Marina showing up and being open to possibilities at the Women's Wisdom event, she met several potential clients for her business. Her follow-up with these individuals led to her first ad sale for the magazine she had just begun to represent, plus a few more business potentials in the pipeline.

We both said yes to opportunity. Marina reminded me, that because I encouraged her to attend, this led to her victorious first sale on her new job! She was elated and grateful. From our initial meeting in person, we discovered our kindred spirit energy while having so much fun connecting and prospering each other in unexpected ways.

Which brings me to another point, when the mojo is flowing, go with the flow of it. When it's not there, don't force it. Walk away. Life is too short to suffer in dead end relationships that don't empower you. Nurturing the good to great relationships is fun and effortless. Don't waste all your time and energy trying so hard on the ones that drain and deplete you. It isn't worth the investment.

Take care of and nurture you first. It frees up your energy and inspiration to create, innovate, collaborate, and radiate the best you possible!

Are you ready to Go Big **AND** Stay Home? Are you ready to invest your time in yourself? How can you balance a full time job and all your other responsibilities with taking care of yourself? Are you ready to have it all? It starts with self-care. When you take care of you first, it frees up energy for you to focus on others.

Set your intention to align with your purpose. Let your heart lead the way to living your life on purpose. Set intentions deliberately to help you stay on track. What's important to you right now in your life? What's important for you to achieve this year and next? What do you want your life to be about?

It is never too late to invest in yourself to build your future. Where are the gaps that need to be addressed and filled to secure the future of your dreams? Do you have a back-up plan? Treat your back-up plan as a marathon. Take it slow and steady and plan and train for it. One day, you will wake up and be glad you took the time to invest in you, even if it takes a bit more discipline and dedication. Be intentional and mindful with each step. Accept your process and learn from your successes and failures.

Make an intentional choice to live your life deliberately and with purpose from your heart.

Just like building a house, you must have a solid foundation to build your network on. It doesn't matter if you're constructing a single-story home or a high-rise in the city. All of the stuff we don't see is the foundation of the building. It's the stuff in the ground, the pre-planning that went into the design, engineering, architecture, innovation, budget, and scheduling in order to build that building. That foundation that we don't see is what makes the building that we do see possible. A strong foundation takes planning and preparation to build. Without the foundation, the building is not possible.

Working in construction for the Walt Disney Company helped me see the importance of building strong foundations. There was a huge project that had been in the planning stages for over ten years. It seemed like it was never going to be built. There were delays in approvals, budgets, timing, etc. Five years after I left the Walt Disney Company, my family and I went to Disneyland for a Thanksgiving Holiday vacation. When we arrived, I was amazed to see the entire project had been built, including a new theme park. California Adventure had hotels, expanded roadways and highways. It was exciting to see that this huge project came to fruition as a result of a collaborative effort and the determination of many people. I cannot imagine the obstacles that team worked through to make that project materialize. The diligence, patience, and dedication of each individual doing their part ultimately caused that monumental project to be completed after over 10 years of planning and waiting.

That story inspires me to be patient about the projects in my life that have been in the concept stage for a long period of time, as I wait for the right time to build the foundation to make them become physical realities in my life. Some projects have come to fruition, like writing this book, and some projects are still in the planning and preparation stage as I wait for approval to begin those projects.

My never-ending life project is to continue to learn how to nurture myself by tuning in to my heart and listen to its guidance. *Peace in my heart means I impart peace unto you.* Asking myself questions helps me find that peace within me and it can help you too. Try some of my favorites:

- **Are my thoughts, words, and actions moving my life forward in a positive direction that's in alignment with my vision?**
- **Is what I am doing healing, building, and empowering my life?**
- **Am I taking the right actions to bring unity to a situation?**
- **Should I learn more about a subject that will enhance my life?**
- **Do I have clarity and courage to take mindful, intentional action?**

Being in a state of positive flow has a magical effect that attracts resources and people to me at the perfect time and place. When challenges arise I move through them while gaining greater wisdom. My life experiences have given me compassion and understanding for others when I see them going through difficult times too. When people are open to support, I try to connect them to resources that may help them move through what may seem like an insurmountable challenge with more ease.

Having the courage to be vulnerable and heartfelt with others has a supernatural affect that encourages them to be vulnerable and heartfelt too. This is when miracles happen, bonds are made, and trust enlivened.

Courage and Vulnerability are the dynamic duo of networking success. It takes courage to go for it. It takes vulnerability to connect with people as your authentic self. It takes courage and vulnerability to make mistakes and keep going. It takes courage to be humble and vulnerable. Having the courage to be vulnerable and connect with others from the heart has a powerful, supernatural effect on others that is contagious. Sometimes other people just need someone else brave enough to lead the way. Courage and vulnerability are the dynamic duo that create bonds, earn trust, and make miracles happen.

I continue to reinforce, acknowledge, and honor myself for the foundation I've built that nurtures my growth and helps me trust that life is working the way it is supposed to. Awareness is the key. It reminds me to breathe, relax, and trust myself on my journey. In this state of being-ness, I am able to be present and open to the flow of divine creativity, serendipity and synchronicity while connecting me to the people, places, and resources I need to be happy and successful. My journey of practicing the art of being versus doing continues as I write this book.

Being open to opportunities makes every day an exciting miracle to live.

Roberto Monaco's Story:

My friend, Roberto Monaco, shared his story at his "Influencing from the Front" workshop I attended. I love Roberto's story because it inspired me to say, "YES!" to life to *Go Big AND Stay Home*. He inspired me to say yes, when I could have said no to opportunities when I wasn't confident about my skills or experience. In order to *Go Big AND Stay Home*, you've got to be willing to say, "YES" to stuff that scares you and forces you out of your comfort zone!

Here's Roberto's story as he tells it:

"I received a call from someone who had met my business partner Jeff, and knew a little bit about what we were doing for clients. This was a referral back in 2009, just after the economy had taken a dive. I was invited to speak at an event in Atlanta, Georgia. It was an opportunity to present in front of over 300 business professionals in the mortgage industry.

I was not paid, nor given any money to cover my travel expenses for airfare, food, and lodging. To top it off, I was also not allowed to sell any of my products at the event. Even though it was not an ideal set up for me, and it was going to cost me money to go, my gut said go for it. So I said, "YES!" and went.

I showed up and the event was a huge success for getting exposure to a captive audience of business professionals. What is so powerful is the domino effect I continue to experience since that event. The connections I made there continue to refer people to me that lead to more opportunities than I could have imagined. That one phone call catapulted my business into high gear and continues to even today! Had I not followed my gut instinct and said, "NO", who knows where my business would be today.

Saying yes that day led to building my business and empowering others to do the same so they could thrive and build their businesses. It provided huge results for my company and my clients. That one event led to paid speaking gigs, filling hundreds of InfluenceOlogy.com workshops, classes, and webinars with cool clients that got to benefit from great results. My business continues to double year after year. I am grateful for such a prosperous life doing what I love to do, empowering people on how to be more influential, whether it's influencing someone one-on-one or influencing one-to-many both online and offline."

Roberto's strategy and biggest take-away is, "You are one presentation away from changing your life. You just don't know which presentation that will be. Show up 100% to all of them, prepared, and on-purpose. Speak to transform versus inform, with passion, skills, and congruency in that moment, to move people towards their goals."

Legendary Roberto Monaco is blazing trails, inspiring the people lucky enough to cross his path, showing up fully and living every day to the fullest! The connections you make and the referrals you receive online and offline have the potential to unleash your business success in unexpected and surprising ways!

Connect with and be mindful of your energy every day. This concept is so powerful. Tune into it by observing how you are experiencing life. This will become the key to unlocking your potential and fulfilling your dreams. It may sound weird to connect to yourself, but it is one of the most empowering gifts you can give yourself. This sets the stage for everything else. Be grateful for all that life has brought you to this day. I have an attitude of gratitude for the gift of life and the people and experiences of my life. The thrill of victory, agony of defeat, and all my life experiences have brought me to where I am and who I am now. Step out of your comfort zone. Do whatever that is for you to live a fuller, richer life!

Plan, navigate, and propel yourself into living life to the fullest. Connect people and resources both online and offline. All the separate components of life, by themselves, serve a singular purpose. The power of putting all the pieces together creates a complete puzzle, a building, a multi-million dollar deal, or helping someone live a fulfilling life.

How to leverage your online or offline presence will vary, depending on where you live and what type of business you own. If you own the only Mexican restaurant in a small town, your customers will most likely come from word-of-mouth and advertising to the local residents. So having a large online marketing campaign would not make much sense. On the other hand, if you are the owner of a Mexican restaurant in San Diego, where there are numerous Mexican restaurants, an online and offline marketing plan is essential so people can find your restaurant easily.

If you have an online business, then an online marketing campaign is critical for your business. You could also do offline marketing via networking events, speaking engagements, and workshops that bring you face-to-face with your client base.

Be strategic and intentional in leveraging both online and offline resources as a smart way to maximize your business success.

Plan your work and work your plan. The synergies of making connections online and in person will help you grow your network exponentially. Create your own strategy and system for connecting and sharing resources with new friends and old, personally and professionally. All the pieces of the puzzle enhance the value and effectiveness of each other when they are combined.

Ch. 2 Recap: Proactive Prosperity

Thought Provoking Questions to Think About

- How are you going to *Go Big AND Stay Home*? What does that mean for you?
- What's your mission? What's your vision? What are your values?
- Have you set up your Success Circles yet?
- What works better for you, Facebook or LinkedIn? Do some research.
- What are the benefits of connecting face-to-face?
- What are the benefits for using technology to leverage your face-to-face connections online?

Mindful Reflections

- Once you've made your initial connection with someone face-to-face, leverage technology to stay connected. There are plenty of online options to connect. Find the ones that work best for you.
- Take care of you first. It frees up your energy to create, collaborate, and innovate with others.
- Set your intention to align with your purpose.
- The dynamic duo of courage and vulnerability has a supernatural effect that is contagious, creates bonds, and earns trust.
- Plan your work and work your plan.
- Build community one Success Circle at a time. Do business with people you like and trust.

Chapter 3:

Harness the Power of Social Media for Your Business

Social Media is here to stay. It has changed the way we connect and communicate. How in the world do you harness the power of social media for your business? What does this mean and why is it important?

The Internet changed everything. It transformed the way we advertise and market our products and services. It has made information more accessible, and as a result, buyers are more informed and sophisticated. Long gone are the simple days of marketing when it only required an average of three contacts to get a buying signal from a prospect. Now it takes at least 8 to 11 marketing touch points on average to get buyers' attention.

Social media channels have rapidly become one of the most popular and effective ways for businesses to advertise and market their products and services. Today's savvy buyers seek out information that helps them make better buying decisions.

Engage them by educating them with meaningful content and a call to action that inspires and motivates them to convert from being prospects into loyal customers.

So how can you succeed using social media to sell your products and services? What are the rules that really work and get results in the social media selling game? Most entrepreneurs are spread thin juggling many priorities and tasks. They know they "should" do more with social media, but they don't. Why? Because they don't understand how to get results with social media that makes it worth their time and effort. Learning how to harness the power of social media is just too overwhelming for a lot of busy entrepreneurs today.

Social media is here to stay. Business owners who bury their heads in the sand and ignore the huge opportunity of social media will be left behind. Social media enables them to expand their marketing efforts exponentially. In order to survive in today's competitive marketplace, small business owners must learn how to harness the power of social media in order to be seen and heard, or they will surely be overlooked and forgotten.

The key to using social media effectively is to have a strategy that drives the eyeballs of your target market to your content. This gets them to your marketing funnel to start the lead conversion process by making offers and calls-to-action. Social selling expands your marketing reach, increases your exposure, and ultimately leads to more sales that keep your business growing and flowing.

There are many businesses that use social media channels effectively. Those businesses that aren't using social media are missing out on many opportunities to attract more prospects.

If you are not using social media to market your business, you are losing business to your competitors who are. You are missing out on opportunities to leverage the most powerful networking tool of the 21st Century - Social Media.

---

11 Excuses Why Businesses Aren't Online

1. **We're too old.**

2. **We're not techy.**

3. **We can't afford it. It's too expensive.**

4. **Privacy, it's not safe or secure.**

5. **It is too complicated.**

6. **We're overwhelmed at the thought of trying to figure it out.**

7. **I'm too busy.**

8. **It won't work for me and my business.**

9. **I don't need to. My competition isn't doing this so why should I?**

10. **I don't understand how it works.**

11. **I don't know who to hire to help me.**

Understanding how to use social media strategies to expand your market exposure and grow your network is no longer optional, but necessary in order to grow your network and your business. It is essential that no matter what industry that you are in, you are the company that is embracing the power of social media marketing. It's important that you integrate many social media channels into your marketing plan for maximum exposure, in order to get ahead of your competition.

UBER, for example, is an innovative on-demand transportation service that has leveraged technology to help get people where they need to go quicker, easier, and cheaper than a taxi. UBER catapulted its way to unimaginable success in just a few short years to become a global phenomenon by leveraging the power of the Internet, Applications, and Social Media.

The Most Popular Social Media Channels today are:
LinkedIn:

Founded in 2003, LinkedIn connects the world's professionals to grow their networks using the power of social media to make them more productive and successful. With more than 430 million members worldwide, including executives from every Fortune 500 Company, LinkedIn is the world's largest professional network on the Internet.

Facebook:

Facebook's mission is to give people the power to share and make the world more open and connected with online social networking. People use Facebook to stay connected and discover what's going on with friends, family, business colleagues, and loyal fans throughout the world.

Twitter:

Twitter is an online social networking service that enables users to send and read short 140-character messages called "tweets." Registered users can read and post tweets. Unregistered users can only read tweets. Users access Twitter through a computer, SMS, or on their cell phones via a mobile device application.

Google+:

Google Inc. launched their social network Google+, in June 2011. Google+ is a place to connect with friends and family, text and video chat called Hangouts, explore interests, share photos, send messages, and stay in touch with the people and topics of interest to you.

YouTube:

Launched in May 2005, YouTube is a global video-sharing website headquartered in San Bruno, California. Google purchased YouTube in November 2006. YouTube allows billions of people to discover, watch, and share originally created videos. YouTube provides a forum for people to connect, inform, and inspire others across the globe and acts as a distribution platform for original content creators and advertisers large and small.

Pinterest:

Pinterest is a photo sharing web and mobile application company that provides a visual discovery and bookmarking tool that enables users to explore, experiment, display, and save creative ideas and projects as an online photo album, scrapbook, or bulletin board.

Instagram:

Instagram is an online mobile photo-sharing, video-sharing, and social networking service that enables users to take pictures and videos, and share them on a variety of social networking platforms, such as Facebook, Twitter, Tumblr, and Flickr. Users can use digital filters to alter or enhance their images. The maximum duration for Instagram videos is only 15-seconds.

Podcasting:

Podcasts are digital audio recordings on a specific area of interest that subscribers can download onto their computer or mobile device.

Apps (Applications):

Applications are computer programs that enable you to add to the abilities of either your computer or laptop's functionality. Mobile apps run on mobile devices, such as smartphones, iPads and tablets. Some apps are free while others need to be purchased in order to have access to them.

Periscope:

This App lets you broadcast and stream live video to the world.

By leveraging these social channels in strategic creative ways, businesses have an impactful new way to create client engagement, community, and loyalty. Successful social media strategies tie into and reflect the company culture. As someone who has done a lot of efforting and pushing through to accomplish important business goals, it is exhilarating to have these tools available at my fingertips now.

Here's a powerful story that showcases the power of leveraging technology. I met Viveka von Rosen, listed as a Forbes Top 20 Women in Social Media (2011–2014) and Forbes Top 50 Most Influential People in Social Media (2011–2014) at the Social Media Marketing World event in San Diego in 2014. She was one of the superstar speakers at the event. I was lucky to have lunch with Viveka one day during the event plus several experts from LinkedIn. I seized the moment and connected with each person on LinkedIn. Since then each individual has been a wonderful resource for me. While writing my book, I thought of experts I could reach out to, to showcase some of their powerful stories. Viveka's story inspired me because, as a result of connecting, referring, and leveraging the power of the Internet, she was able to set off a chain of events that had a huge impact on her life and many people's lives in her network!

Viveka von Rosen tells her story:

"My story starts with the KING of connection, Mr. Bob Burg himself! I had been referring Bob's book, *The Go-Giver* and his "Endless Referrals" program for years, but it never occurred to me to reach out to him. I mean he was BOB BURG and I was some business office manager. One day, on Twitter, (I can picture myself, my desk, and my computer perfectly),

I just threw the tweet out there, "Does anyone know if Bob Burg is on Twitter?" This was back in 2009, before Twitter's search engine was really working.

Well, not only did Mr. Bob Burg (@BobBurg) himself reply to me, but he followed me so that I could private message him. In a series of private messages, he agreed to let me interview him for our blog, and we became "social friends."

After the interview, Bob and I stayed in touch. One day I was thrilled to see another message from Bob inviting me to his event in Florida. A friend of mine and I went to his 3-day event, where I met some of the people who would later help me grow my career, Nathan Latka, Mari Smith, Rebel Brown, Trey Pennington, and Kimberly Bohannon. Never estimate the power of one tweet. Hey, does anyone know if ???? is on Twitter, or LinkedIn, or Facebook, or Periscope or Instagram or Pinterest or … ?"

What I love about this industry is the kindness from the people at the top of their game, and how they are willing to help you on your journey of connecting, referring, and creating your road to riches! They love connecting and being connected! At the core of all this technology is the power of caring from the heart about people. You can feel that, even through the Internet, and especially when you meet them in person.

The Internet has created a paradigm shift in how businesses market themselves today. You don't have to push through the front door to get customers anymore. You can attract clients to you like bees to honey with enticing and engaging content and calls-to-action that convert prospects into customers online.

Social Media is a way to form a relationship with a broader audience in order to expand your list of contacts and customers. Finding a way to relate and make the customer experience richer, easier and more fun is an ongoing process! For example, Starbucks is the company to watch when it comes to effective marketing. They have an endless list of creative marketing ideas that they continue to wow and woo their customers with. How many of their ideas can you put to use in your retail business? What are you doing that Starbucks is not doing? How many ideas that work in one industry will transfer to another? If you are the first to try a new concept and it works, how big will your advantage be?

**Social media has harnessed the power of the Internet to create a global marketplace that never sleeps. Successful social media strategies attract and convert leads into customers while you sleep.
Now that's my idea of leverage!**

Here are some concerns and questions about how social media works:
- **Where do I start?**
- **How much will this cost?**
- **Who do I trust to help me with this?**

It can be a daunting undertaking to try to figure out which social media channels are the best ones for your business needs. How do you implement social selling? Research and interview experts until you find the ones that work for you.

Social Media Misconceptions and Easy Fixes:

Unrealistic Expectations: Are you generating revenue from new clients and loyal fans from social media channels? Don't drop the traditional marketing channels like email, phone calls, direct mail, since they are all important to increase your odds in generating revenue. Use them all to turn your business into a marketing machine.

Time Sucker: Is social media sucking time out of your day? Are you consumed with posting and monitoring your social media? Schedule your social media time. Discipline yourself to stick to your posting schedule. You only need to spend 30-minutes a day posting on social media, either in the morning or evening, to be effective. That's it!

Social Media Channel to Email List: Have you captured your clients, fans, and followers from the social media channels you are marketing on? Since the social media rules and regulations are ever changing, make sure to download your contacts to a spreadsheet or customer relationship management (CRM) database regularly. Think of this as an insurance policy for your contact list.

Consistency Commitment: Are you posting daily or weekly? Do you have a social media marketing strategy for consistent exposure?

Engage: How are you engaging your audience? Are you posting interesting content, inspirational quotes, doing a survey, creating audience participation by asking them questions, offering access to info by signing up to receive updates?

Listen: Are you taking time to listen to your clients' wants and needs? Take a breath. Kick back. Take some time out to tune in and listen to what your customers are asking for. Then reply. Good customer service is when you are willing to face any problem and find a solution that makes your customer happy. Your customers will appreciate that you care enough to listen to them and respond to solve their problems.

Value: Are you providing content that is valuable to your target market? How do you think your customer feels when reading the content you are providing? Are you providing relevant content that educates and empowers them to make buying decisions? Is it useful to them?

The fastest and most efficient way to streamline your learning curve and launch your social media presence is to hire an expert who specializes in the social media channel you've chosen to market your business through. You can add other channels later. If you want to implement an extensive social media marketing plan quickly and have the marketing budget for it, hire an on-line digital marketing company that has expertise in all the social media channels.

Social media marketing is not a get rich quick marketing solution for your business. Like anything of value, it takes time to build. It requires an investment and commitment in order to reap the rewards. Decide on a place to start. Be consistent. Monitor your progress. Record results like new contacts and increased sales.

Start with at least one social media channel and build from there. What's important is to start somewhere and get in the game. Implement a "how to" plan to harness the power of social media for your business. Then go for it. Get online to get linked in and connected.

**Social media channels leverage the
global marketplace on the Internet
to expand your reach beyond what is
humanly possible in person.**

How to choose the social channel that's right for you and your business:

Q: Are you a business professional?
A: Get on LinkedIn to establish credibility, connect to other professionals, and look for job opportunities.

Q: Are you a woman's clothing boutique owner?

A: Use Facebook to connect and sell primarily to women.

Q: Are you a speaker, trainer, or a coach?
A: Use YouTube videos to showcase your expertise, style, and skill.

Q: Are you a college student with a photography business?
A: Use Instagram or Pinterest to promote your visual photography business.

Q: Are you a person of few words who likes to keep it brief?
A: Use Twitter to send your message in 140 characters or less.

Q: How do famous people, movie stars, pop vocalist stay connected with fans?
A: Twitter or Instagram

Q: How do investors, day-traders, and analysts receive timely news and events?
A: Twitter!

How much money should you budget for your marketing? The U.S. Small Business Administration recommends a marketing budget of 7–8% if your gross annual revenue is $5 million or less. The percentage depends on your industry and the size of your company.

Use a ballpark figure to estimate your marketing budget. **Ask yourself these simple questions:**

- **How much profit will one sale generate?**
- **How long is my sales cycle?**
- **How quickly can I recoup my marketing investment?**
- **What are my competitors doing?**
- **What funds do I have available to spend on social media marketing right now?**

Depending on the complexities of your business, there may be many more factors to take into consideration.

Different industries have different budgets for marketing. A realtor is going to have a different marketing budget than a pet sitter.

There are sophisticated systems online for tracking and recording Social Media marketing results to determine if they are achieving the results you desire.

Search Engine Optimization (SEO) is a visibility ranking on the Internet. When you have good SEO ranking for your website and social media profiles, it means you have good visibility. Social Media marketing helps enhance your SEO rankings.

SEO is a rapidly shifting and changing business that is difficult to keep up with. The rules are always changing. There are companies that specialize in SEO to help improve your online visibility. Buyer beware. There are a lot of SEO scams out there. Research and review before hiring someone.

An SEO data report helps you market smarter, because it reveals trends, like how people are getting to your website, how long they are staying engaged, where they are bouncing off your website.

SEO experts can use the data report to create strategic solutions for redesigning your website and social media marketing campaign to increase user-engagement, minimize bounce rates, and maximize traction with calls-to-action for converting visitors to your website to potential clients.

**Is your current marketing strategy
attracting more clients
and increasing your customer loyalty and cash flow?**

The bottom line that everyone wants to know is, will social media marketing increase my visibility on the Internet? Yes, it most definitely will. That's what this book is all about. Social media has helped me grow my online presence and increased my visibility and contact list of my clients too. It can work for you and your business too.

It's amazing to me what having an online presence can do for your business. Before the Internet, if a company was local it flourished through word of mouth referrals plus the traditional methods of marketing, newspaper, radio and TV ads, which are expensive. With the Internet, this same local company has the opportunity to create a global presence by launching an online presence via social media channels, which are free. People from around the world, who have Internet access, can find your business and visit it. The Internet has created a global marketplace in which you can find anything, anywhere, from anyone in the world. That is so fascinating to me. I feel incredibly lucky to be living during such an exciting time.

By leveraging the power of relationship marketing via word of mouth, the Internet, websites, and social media channels, a company has the potential to go from local to global practically overnight.

Make a choice to get started with a digital marketing solution today. Save yourself time, money, and frustration by hiring a social media expert to help you, rather than trying to figure it out on your own. You are the expert in your business, so that's where you should focus your time and energy rather than trying to figure out the ever-changing world of online marketing. Be smart and outsource to the pros who specialize in social media marketing and can set you up to win. This is critical to your online success, so you are free to focus your time and energy on what you do best, your business.

The question is, how do you know which expert to trust and hire to set up, optimize, and grow your online presence via the many social media channels? Reach out to your network and find out. Find resources via referrals from people who have already used the services needed. I have included a list of references in the Resources section, at the back of this book. I've used my network and done the due diligence for you by providing quality contacts that will fast track your networking to get results quickly. If you can't find what you're looking for there, email me. I will help you find a resource that can help you.

Here are some suggestions on how to find the resources you need to set up your online marketing. Start by creating a checklist of criteria that are important to you for hiring an outsourced solution. Ask your business associates if they have access to or experience working with any online digital marketing companies. Check in with both your online and offline networks.

There are several ways to reach out online. You could send an email, connect on LinkedIn or Facebook, or send a text message to their phone. You can do research online, in order to set up face-to-face meetings and interviews with local companies in your area. You can connect offline through face-to-face meetings and networking groups. Be open to virtual consults as an option when you are considering companies not in your geographic area.

Do your due diligence to find the Internet marketing company that's right for you and your business. This requires a combination of talking with your network, researching companies on-line, reviewing LinkedIn profiles to see how you and your network are connected, and researching the different options available in your area. Third party testimonials and recommendations are a great resource for your research. Check out client testimonials on Yelp, and recommendations on LinkedIn. Once you have done your homework, select two to three companies, schedule interviews with each one to find out who is the best fit for your company.

**Hire a digital marketing company that creates
a turnkey social media strategy that is a
sustainable and cost effective solution for you.**

During "Social Media Marketing World 2015", hosted in San Diego by Social Media Examiner, the hot topic was about how important video is in your online marketing today. Michael Stelzner, the host of the event, reported that video is the most powerful tool to use on all the social media channels. "Native video is an untapped frontier, 57% of marketers are using video, 72% plan on increasing use of video and want to learn more, a small percentage of marketers are using Instagram, 36% (15-second videos), Vine 4% (6-second videos) and Snapchat 2%." There are also new tools like Twitter's Periscope to live stream our lives and businesses.

According to Hubspot, "People are 44% more likely to engage with content on social media that contains pictures. Creating visual content takes more time and resources." Simply put, video drives traffic because it engages people. The power of being able to create a video from our handheld devices, like the iPhone or iPad, and post immediately to the social media channels is efficient and effective. It's perfect for the world of technology and instant gratification we live in today.

I've discovered that many entrepreneurs and businesses have archives of audio and video collecting dust. Videos are a wealth of content that aren't being monetized like they could be. I have a solution.

The problem with video is that people become self-conscious and worry about how they look or question if they are good looking or professional enough to create their own video. If you are camera shy you have several options. First, take the spotlight off yourself and focus on your audience. Give them the information they are eager to receive. Next, hire a stylist for a makeover to update your professional image or hire a spokesperson for your company. Most importantly, take action, and move forward.

Transcribe your videos and get them out there before your competition beats you to it. Use a video to tell a story and show the bigger picture. Publish it on your website and all your social media channels to increase views and drive traffic to your website. Make sure it is entertaining and engaging.

Transcribed content can be re-purposed and used on all the social media channels. Your digital marketing team can take care of the transcription process and posting your video on all your social media channels for you.

The result of using this content in your social video marketing strategy is that it has the power to exponentially increase the impact of your marketing message, creating increased brand awareness, loyal following, and ultimately increased sales. I have a superb team of experts who have the ability do all this and more! Be sure to check out the "Resources" section at the back of the book.

Social Media is the rocket fuel your business needs to soar to new heights of success. Here's why, It is:

- **Innovative**
- **Comprehensive**
- **Streamlines and expedites your marketing efforts**
- **Systemizes your ability to track online sales conversions**
- **Optimizes lead generation**

- **Leverages strategic alliances**
- **Influences prospects to make buying decisions**
- **Converts prospects into customers**
- **Can be monetized to create multiple streams of income**

You and your business will be reaping the rewards of your efforts with the Social Media tool chest.

I have put together a roadmap to guide you on your Social Media exploration and implementation. It is your turn to take action, have fun, and leverage the resources I'm providing to you in this book.

1st. **READY: Social Media and Marketing Assessment**
2nd. **AIM: Evaluate where you are today and where you want to be**
3rd. **FIRE: Implement a plan of action to achieve your goals**

Ch. 3 Recap: Proactive Prosperity

Thought Provoking Questions to Think About

- How are you going to *Go Big AND Stay Home*? What does that mean for you?
- What are your reasons for not doing business online? If you aren't, your customers are, and so are your competitors.
- Have you found the social media channel that's right for you?

Mindful Reflections

- If you are not using social media to advertise your business, you are losing business to your competitors who are.
- Social media channels leverage the global marketplace on the Internet to expand your reach beyond what is humanly possible in person.
- The top social channels available today include: LinkedIn, Facebook, Twitter, Google+, YouTube, Pinterest, Instagram, Podcasting & Apps.
- Successful social media strategies attract and convert leads into customers while you sleep. Now that's my idea of leverage!

Chapter 4:

Magic of Linking Online

I am fascinated by how magical and synergistic getting linked in to someone online can be. Grow your network exponentially one person at a time in order to elevate your business success to new heights. Business Professionals use LinkedIn, Facebook, or both, to leverage the power of social media marketing.

Comparing LinkedIn and Facebook is like comparing apples and oranges. Both are effective channels for social selling.
LinkedIn is for professionals who want to grow their professional network and establish credibility. Use Facebook to grow your personal network and market products or services.
Use them strategically and synergistically to expand your connections and visibility.

If you aren't on either one of these channels it's time to get online to grow your network. Embrace technology and get connected to your network online now. Get connected to your professional network and watch it grow as your reputation blossoms through LinkedIn. You can use LinkedIn to establish credibility, position yourself as an expert in your field, and grow your professional network.

Connect with your personal network of family and friends on Facebook. Even though it is mainly for personal connections, it can also help supercharge your business. Your personal relationships have the potential to lead you to unexpected resources for your business.

Leveraging these two popular social channels is a smart start to going online to expand your network. Over time, you can add the other social media channels as needed, as referenced in Chapter 3.

Having a social media presence increases your visibility and accessibility to prospects 24 hours a day, 365 days a year. It enhances your face-to-face connections, which are limited to certain hours and days during the work week. LinkedIn and Facebook are popular social media channels you can use to expand your exposure to attract new clients and a loyal following of friends and fans to your business.

Whether you are an individual realtor, small business owner, or a Fortune 500 company, there are strategies for leveraging each social media channel to fuel your marketing pipeline with solid leads for a loyal client base. Is your competition posting to all the social channels or one specific channel? Is your company the leader in your industry and paving the way for the other companies? Find out what your competition is doing and either do it better or do something unique that sets you apart. Social media can help you be creative about how you present your brand online.

I understand how overwhelming it all can be. The challenge of being overwhelmed is that it often renders us inactive. We end up not taking action because we don't know where to start. However, when you take some action, no matter how small it helps reduce overwhelm and empowers you in the process. When you step up and out of your comfort zone, it is good for your self-confidence, as well as your business.

I have made it a practice to surround myself with thought leaders and experts in the world of Social Media. At times it has been overwhelming to me, as I learned about this new and exciting online world of social media networking and marketing. But now, as a result of researching and attending events where the social media thought leaders were speaking and seizing the moment to meet them after their presentations, I know who to go to for the cutting edge insights. I am willing to invest in learning, in order to replace overwhelm with empowerment. I am here to help you do the same. Check out the "Resources" section to help you get started networking and marketing your business online. Take action today to replace overwhelm with the empowerment of learning a new cost effective way to market your business online.

It is impossible for one person to know everything.
It is possible to learn something new every day.
Learn how to use one social media channel first.
Then add others later after you have mastered one.

One of my favorite annual events, Social Media Marketing World hosted by SocialMediaExaminer.com, bustles with the heavy hitters in Social Media who speak, share their wisdom and experience, network, and hang out. They are approachable, helpful, and generous about answering questions to help you better understand the possibilities of what social media can do for you and your business.

The Social Media Marketing World event is a fantastic way to meet and make new connections with these incredible thought leaders. I met Mari Smith, the Face of Facebook, in 2002, before social media was even popular yet. Over the years we lost contact with each other, then twelve years later we reconnected. Shortly before she was about to go on stage to speak to a ballroom full of attendees at the Social Media Marketing World 2014 event we bumped into each other in the ladies room. She sent me a Facebook friend request just before going on stage! It was as if no time had passed since we saw each other last. I share this example because Mari Smith is a world-renowned Social Media thought leader and premiere Facebook expert. What is amazing about Mari is that not only is she a gorgeous brilliant human being, she has a huge loving heart and cares about people. I am honored to have her as a dear friend in my life.

At the same event that day, my business partner Christopher and I set out to mingle and have lunch with the LinkedIn Company Representatives attending the event. Not only did we have lunch with them, Viveka von Rosen, a LinkedIn rock star joined us too! It was better than I could have hoped for. She was what I aspired to become. I was so excited to be spending time with her and the LinkedIn team because that is my favorite social media channel that I had chosen to specialize in. Now I am connected with all of them on LinkedIn. They have proven to be a valuable resource that I can reach out to for help with a question, or just to stay connected with a simple "Hi" or "Thank You for all your help."

I have another fun story to share as a result of attending the Social Media Marketing World 2015 event. At the kick-off party, I was hanging out with Mari and Christopher on the USS Midway, an aircraft carrier housing a maritime museum located in downtown San Diego at the Navy Pier. Mari introduced me to Ron Nash, another LinkedIn expert. In fact, he is known as the "LinkedIn Whisperer." We had a blast connecting and talking about life. Since then we've connected on LinkedIn. I have reached out to him for help and to gain a better understanding of certain LinkedIn features. He spent time with me to ensure I was prepared for an upcoming client meeting. I was honored and grateful for every second of his time and every bit of knowledge I learned from him. The time he spent with me set me up for greater success in supporting my clients. He's an amazing, intelligent, and fun human being with the kindest heart and people's best interest top of mind.

Thought Leaders in the Social Media industry are accessible, generous, and helpful. They continue to figure out "Social Selling" and fearlessly guide the way, navigating unchartered waters and discovering smart, savvy business solutions for all to benefit from.

Based on my client's needs, I have an arsenal of savvy business resources to guide them on their Social Media

Marketing adventure. Synergistic business partnerships empower each of us to focus on our core expertise. When I assess a client's needs, I start with LinkedIn for their business. In the process, I determine what the next steps should be to expand their social media presence.

I take my clients through a process of connecting intentionally and strategically within their network, both in person and on LinkedIn. On many occasions, a significant contact is made with a key person who they did not even realize was a "missing link" for their business. Re-connecting with friends and colleagues you've lost touch with is one of the greatest benefits of social media. It helps you find people you've lost track of and get reconnected.

Social media is the quickest and easiest way to reconnect with lost contacts. When you do get reconnected with someone who has been missing from your life for a long time, it's empowering and fun to restore those heart-to-heart connections. Social media works like magic for finding the lost people in your life while also finding new friends and business associates to grow your network as well. Social media helps you create win-win connections with old friends and new alike.

**Unleash the power of face-to-face
connections by getting Linked In online.**

I met my wonderful friend Kathryn almost ten years ago when I was interviewing Feng Shui experts to speak at an event I was creating for Realtors. She has taught me so much about Classical Feng Shui over the years. Every year I hire Kathryn to give my home and office a Feng Shui reboot. She helps me set up my furniture to enhance all areas of my life with the specific protocols of the Chinese New Year.

At the end of the year 2014, I called Kathryn for a consult to work her magic in our new place in Del Mar. I wanted to be prepared for the New Year. Kathryn, Reed, and I went to work moving our furnishings around until they were in the best possible spots to enhance our lives. It was an amazing and profound experience. It made such a positive difference to the energy and feeling in our home. It reduced the stress in our lives by creating a sanctuary of our home!

Prior to this, the layout of our master bedroom was preventing us from getting a good night's sleep. We were challenged with disappointments and unexpected failures in our lives as well. So we made some changes. In fact, we actually moved our master bedroom to a completely different room. Then we relocated my home office space into the old master bedroom. It was amazing what a difference that made almost immediately. Both rooms felt more harmonious. We started sleeping more soundly and my office environment shifted from a constricting space to a beautiful open and expansive space for prospering.

We had almost skipped our annual Feng Shui tune up but were glad we didn't because we could feel the difference almost immediately. After noticing the difference that last session made, we committed never to miss our annual Feng Shui tune up again. We are so grateful for Kathryn's Feng Shui expertise and her wealth of wisdom that makes our lives work so much better.

As a result of reconnecting with Kathryn, she hired me to coach her on maximizing LinkedIn for her businesses—classical

Feng Shui and residential real estate. Through the work we did together in strategically positioning her LinkedIn profile, intentionally navigating, connecting, and marketing her business, she reconnected with a long lost business friend in international banking. As a result of them reconnecting, they became referral partners for each other. They were so grateful to have rekindled their friendship. It's amazing to witness how the power of one person can shift your whole outlook on life from lackluster to re-energized, re-igniting your passion for what you do.

Kathryn shared the following with me.

> "I'm working smarter and more effectively. Through your LinkedIn coaching, I've been reminded how the power of connecting with my network really can be life changing. I now understand the power of building my referral partners for qualified leads and how LinkedIn is an effective tool to do that."

My dear friend Dr. Steven Ross, also has a success story about how social media helped his business. Dr. Ross and I met in 2006, when I was in search of a holistic health practitioner. I met a lady at the grocery store. She invited me to attend an event Dr. Ross was speaking at about Chiropractic care with a specialty in Integrated and Functional Medicine. After attending that event, I started seeing Dr. Ross. Through his care and guidance, we were able to restore my health so I felt great again.

When he found out I was providing LinkedIn business consulting, he hired me to help him with his LinkedIn profile. This is the testimonial he shared on LinkedIn about the work we did together to get him linked in:

"During my initial strategy session with Tracie, I had a pivotal moment that created great clarity about my life purpose. I made a decision to honor what caused me to look deep inside and develop my profile as a Speaker, Author, Educator, and Entrepreneur, who is making a difference in people's health by educating doctors and patients about my passion, Integrated & Functional Medicine.

Through our strategy sessions, I was able to reconnect with my life's passion. There was one key person in my network, Tracie Hasse, who brought me awareness of LinkedIn as a powerful networking source and contact management system.

Thank you again for all you do Tracie, and for the terrific education you gave me through our LinkedIn strategy sessions. Your guidance has really simplified navigating LinkedIn. I am leveraging my contacts with purpose and intention. You have opened my vision to the many opportunities through LinkedIn as a key marketing channel for me. Thank You Tracie!"

Amy has another social media success story. Amy and I met through real estate in 2007. She has always been tech savvy and explored all the social media channels. She had been on LinkedIn for a few years, accepting invitations to connect. She already had over 1,500 connections but wasn't using LinkedIn intentionally. When we got together in our strategy session, it was a huge eye opener for Amy, since she did not realize the power of LinkedIn.

The following weekend I received a call from her that went something like this:

"Tracie, I am so excited. As a result of our strategy session and really understanding the power of LinkedIn and connecting with my network, I reconnected with a dear friend from high school, Melissa. We had lunch together to catch up and reconnect. As it turns out, we live five minutes from each other and she is a small business attorney. We will be referring clients to each other and she is hiring me to list her home when she is ready to sell. Thank You for educating and empowering me about the power of LinkedIn.

Your strategies for lead generation through LinkedIn are genius! Implementing these changes has opened up a new channel of communication to make connections that are more powerful, productive, and professional than Facebook or Twitter. By connecting the dots of people in my network, I am learning to navigate through my many contacts to find those most likely to engage in business for my real estate services. I am thrilled after a few tweaks, some focus, and an open mind. Tracie, you are unlocking the mystery known as LinkedIn!"

With these individuals, it all started with each one of them making a decision to be on LinkedIn and most importantly, use LinkedIn to reach business goals. If you are not on LinkedIn for your business, the time to let your presence be known is now. It is free so you have no excuse. If you don't have time to figure it out, I highly recommend hiring a LinkedIn specialist to help you. In 2011, I hired a business coach that specialized in LinkedIn to help me expedite and streamline how to use LinkedIn.

Because LinkedIn is a key social media channel for business professionals, it is an integral part of my consulting business. A business coach who specializes in LinkedIn can guide you and streamline your efforts to establish a professional presence on LinkedIn. They can educate you on implementing a marketing campaign to take advantage of the treasure trove of secrets within LinkedIn and help you create smart strategies for using LinkedIn to leverage your connections.

**"LinkedIn is rich in opportunity flow
because relationships matter!"**

~ Reid Hoffman, Co-Founder LinkedIn

Set Yourself Up for Success BEFORE you start Expert Positioning your LinkedIn Profile by doing the following:

- *Turn-OFF "Notify Your Network" on Right side of your Profile screen; Once profile complete, Turn-ON to "Notify Your Network"*

- *Use a WORD Document for creating your content, then cut-&-paste into LinkedIn profile. It's smart to have a back-up of your content.*

- *Be Consistent with transferring your Brand message from existing Website to LinkedIn profile if you have a website.*

11 Secrets to Expert Position Your LinkedIn Profile + BONUS Secret:

1. Add a BANNER, located at the top of your LinkedIn Profile, to make your Profile stand out. Create a premier banner with your logo, tagline, and keywords. Position the words across the top, left, and right sections of the banner so they are visible, since your photo, name & professional header section take up a portion of the banner area. LinkedIn Banner specs: Use a JPG, PNG, or GIF under 4MB in size. A resolution of 1400 by 425 pixels looks best.

2. Add an Up-to-date "Professional Headshot Photo". If you don't have a photo your profile is more likely to be skipped over.

3. Create a catchy, keyword rich, top-notch professional headline. This is equivalent to your 10-second elevator pitch, plus this is what shows up in searches along with your photo.

4. Complete your "Contact" information so people know how to reach you.

5. In your "Summary" section include who you are and what you do, who you work with, the problem/pain you help your clients solve, and why/how you make a difference with your expertise. You have 2,000 character spaces available here.

   Add Rich media: document, photo, link, video, presentation.

6. Complete the "Experience" section thoroughly by filling in all the boxes. That way if people search for you by the previous company where you both worked, your profile will show up so they can find you.

   Add Rich media: document, photo, link, video, presentation

7. "Recommendations" can be Given and Requested. It is critical to give them to the people in your network and ask for them from your clients to add to your profile.

8. In the "Skills and Endorsements" section include keywords you want to be found by relevant to your expertise.

9. Add your Education, Certifications, and Organizations since people may be searching for you this way too.

10. Add "Advice for Contacting You." Let people know the best way to contact you. Include your phone number and/or email. Add a note inviting them to connect with you on LinkedIn and a call to action to click on a link to take them to your website.

11. Find Groups to Join and Create Your own Groups relevant to your interests and target market for your business. Request to join them. Create conversations. Ask questions. Have fun building relationships that lead to business opportunities.

BONUS:
Leverage LinkedIn by using it as a key marketing channel. Create a Marketing Campaign on LinkedIn to showcase you and your business. Write your own Posts. Add media to your profile in addition to written content. Photos, links, videos, and presentations enhance the visibility of your profile. This is important for people to get to know you, your business, and to build community and a loyal fan base.

LinkedIn rates your Profile strength on your Profile page. You can see this by going to your profile. When in edit mode, it shows your profile strength on the right hand column of your page. The stronger your profile is the higher your rating becomes. The higher your profile rating is, the higher your visibility on LinkedIn becomes. It is worth the time invested to create a strong profile because this is your launch pad for marketing you.

I have put together a methodology I use to teach clients how to understand and use LinkedIn in an intentional way that gets results. Just like websites, it is important to use the keywords you want people to find you by within your profile so it is optimized for the highest visibility. A strong profile is keyword rich. Learn the basics to strategically increase your marketing success using LinkedIn. Here's how:

Checklist to Strategically Leverage LinkedIn:

- Showcase you, your expertise in your LinkedIn profile. Use keywords that help people find you for what you want to be found for.
- Navigate LinkedIn intentionally with the purpose of optimizing and leveraging your LinkedIn presence and connections.
- Evaluate whether or not you should "Accept Invitation" or "Ignore Invitation" to connect. Do you know the person? Who are your mutual shared connections? Do you have potential business synergies with what they do? If yes, "Accept". If none of these apply and the person is 100% selling you with no interest in you, "Ignore". This is your Invitation Only Database. You decide who's in or out.
- Create personalized templates for "Invitations" and/or "Requests to Connect"; this sets you apart from the majority of people who do not take the time to do this. Possibly share how you could be a resource for them, and ask how you could help them.

- Use Spiral Mapping to **tag** your network for "Quality" connections vs. "Quantity" and to organize your connections.

- Master Mine Your Network to create referral partners and strategic alliances for lead generation pipelines.

- Use LinkedIn as your customer relationship management (CRM) database to systematize your network by tagging connections, adding client notes, and scheduling follow-up reminders.

- When questions arise use the "HELP Center" for solutions. Put your cursor over the tiny photo of you in the upper right-hand corner when logged into your LinkedIn Profile. A dropbox will appear, click on "Help Center".

- Use LinkedIn as your marketing channel. Write your own posts. These land on your Home Page Profile as your "Posts." Review articles, event postings, and other sources of information frequently. Understand the top needs, concerns, problems, and goals of your ideal clients to help create an effective marketing strategy.

Click on the numerous icons in LinkedIn to find resources, tools, and short cuts to organize and leverage your network. Post consistently versus randomly to build trust, to attract a following of people who eventually may become customers or referral partners.

Using LinkedIn effectively is not about connecting with hundreds and hundreds of people for the sake of connecting. People get hung up on not having 500+ first degree connections on LinkedIn and feel like they are not using it properly, or not at all, because they do not know that many people. Focus on creating **Quality** connections versus **Quantity**. It is a better investment of your time and efforts.

It only takes a few key people in your network to help boost your success. If I had my current network, plus a few of my favorite people, like Tony Robbins, Oprah Winfrey, Richard Branson, Madonna, Deepak Chopra, Panache Desai, I would be connected to a phenomenal global network. For me this would be a dream come true network. It doesn't have to be that many people to be powerful. Dream big! That's where it starts.

A powerful network is one that helps you overcome challenges by connecting you to resources and people for collaboration to get things done, no matter what the size of the problem or project.

I did this on LinkedIn and you can too. Do you have someone on your wish list that you would like to connect with and meet? Here is how you can do that using LinkedIn. Remember, some people are on LinkedIn and some are not. I happen to have a few people on my wish list who are on LinkedIn.

Start by typing in the person's name you want to connect with, in the LinkedIn search bar at the top on the screen. If they are on LinkedIn, their profile box will appear on your screen, so click on this box. Once you're on their Profile scroll down to see how you are connected with this person by looking at your Connections.

I have a few 1st degree connections in my network that are also 1st degree connections with my wish list people. Therefore, I have a 2nd degree connection to my wish list connections, Tony Robbins and Deepak Chopra.

Next, reach out to your 1st degree connection in your network that has a connection with the person you want to meet. Ask if they would set up an introduction for you with the person you want to meet. Add a personal touch with a call and email to your 1st degree connection, to express your appreciation. Don't be afraid to make these connections. Reach out to your network and have fun in the process.

On LinkedIn, you have the ability to see how you are connected to people through 1st, 2nd, and 3rd degree connections. There are "Three Degrees of Connection" for getting to know people on LinkedIn. The movie, *Six Degrees of Separation,* also illustrates the point that we are all more closely connected than we realize. The Internet and social media channels such as LinkedIn and Facebook have created an even more closely connected world.

In an effort to clear up any misunderstandings about what LinkedIn is and what it isn't, I have included some clarifications below. Let's start with what LinkedIn is not.

11 Things LinkedIn is NOT:

1. **A Dating Site**

2. **A Resume Service**

3. **A place for one-sided selling**

4. **A place to make useless connections with strangers for no reason**

5. **A venue for spamming people**

6. **An employment agency**

7. **A waste of time**

8. **Expensive**

9. **Useless**

10. **A personal place for sharing photos of your social life**

11. **Facebook or Twitter**

Don't listen to the gossip about what people think LinkedIn is or isn't. Experience it for yourself to draw your own conclusions. The only way to find out if it will benefit you is to try it out for yourself. When I discovered LinkedIn, I got it right away because I thought to myself, *Wow, this is the visual of how my mind works when networking and connecting people together.*

On LinkedIn, you are able to see photos of people and how you are connected through mutual connections. I thought this was brilliant, since there is no way to know the extent of these connections through face-to-face conversations. When I discovered LinkedIn I did not have time to figure it out. I hired a coach to streamline my learning curve to put this phenomenal tool into action right away.

LinkedIn is a key foundational social channel for entrepreneurs and business professionals. If you are not on LinkedIn and don't have the time to learn how to use it through trial and error, hire a specialist like me to speed up your learning curve and get you on the road to riches as soon as possible. We can work together one-on-one or through workshops to show you how to use LinkedIn. LinkedIn helps you attract, nurture, and grow connections in your network to increase the success of your business and your network's business. Now let's look at what LinkedIn is.

11 Secrets about what LinkedIn IS:

1. **A secret weapon for business professionals**

2. **Your marketing channel to the business world**

3. **Top business professionals networking site**

4. **The social media channel to connect with your coworkers and build brand awareness**

5. **The place to influence the market with your expertise**

6. **A stealth way to prepare for business meetings and interviews**

7. **A place to Post your valuable marketing content consistently and intentionally to attract business and loyal clients**

8. **An Invitation-Only database in which you have control over who you invite to connect with and whose invitation you decide to accept.**

9. **A Customer Relationship Management (CRM) database of your connections to optimize your network to be more effective**

10. **A virtual way to get introduced via your network to other business professionals**

11. A smart tool to leverage for building strategic alliances and referral partners for lead generation

---

"LinkedIn is 277% more effective for lead generation than Facebook or Twitter."

~ Hubspot

Unleash the power of face-to-face networking with your online digital marketing to generate even more business. LinkedIn is your "Go-To" Marketing Channel. It capitalizes on your in-person relationships to create a powerful synergy that optimizes and leverages your network to create a system of success and prosperity for all to benefit from.

LinkedIn is the world's largest professional network with an international presence, focused expertise, and cooperative mindset of business professionals. With the LinkedIn network, you have a powerful resource for building brand awareness, attracting clients, and showcasing you and your company. On LinkedIn, people can find you while you sleep!

"Chance favors the connected mind and puts you one step closer to game changing opportunities!"

~ Reid Hoffman, Co-Founder LinkedIn

My interview with Ron Nash showcases this quote. Ron Nash is known as the LinkedIn Whisperer. Founder of *Jump Start Academy Global*, Ron Nash is an entrepreneur and an inspirational coach with a focus on business and career.

For over 20 years, he has worked with clients from LinkedIn, Microsoft, T-Mobile, Samsung, and The Anthony Robbins Companies. Ron has also collaborated with celebrities like Cesar Millan - The Dog Whisperer, Deepak Chopra, Eckhart Tolle, Carlos Santana, and Don Miguel Ruiz.

Ron Nash Interview

Tracie Hasse: Ron, today I'd like to interview you for my book, *Go Big AND Stay Home.* I'd love to hear one of your stories.

Ron Nash: Number one, I commend you for your book and what you are doing. This is a great story. It is a story that needs to be told. There are a number of things that I can talk about in terms of the way things have happened for me as I create my life.

I am a co–creator with this wonderful universe. So many really amazing things are happening. About two-and-half years ago, I had already written two books. One of the last books I wrote was called *Leveraging LinkedIn: The Essential Guide to your Career Network.*

I had been speaking quite a bit. There was a group of close friends in Northern California that invited me to speak at one of their networking groups.

Ron Nash: It was such a cool opportunity so I decided to take them up on it. Waiting for my flight in the airport, I got distracted on the phone with a friend and missed my flight (laughing). So I decided to catch the next one, but I didn't realize they only had one flight a day going there. They had promoted this event a month in advance. Everybody was excited about it.

I called the promoter to tell him I missed my flight. He was great about it but I could tell he was disappointed. I checked other airlines for a flight. I was able to get a flight and some friends picked me up and got me to the event on time. It was standing room only, with over 100 people there. I had so much fun! (laughs).

It was so cool because I received so much energy back from them from what I gave. I ended up doing a raffle and gave away one coaching package. It was going so well and I was feeling so good, I thought, "Yeah, what the heck. I'm feeling good. I'm going to raffle off five more" (Laughs). The energy was pouring in and we had such a great time.

A lot of people received gifts, which was my intended outcome. There was one guy who received a coaching package and actually followed through to retrieve it.

He almost didn't make it there. After the first coaching session, he said, "Hey, Ron, are you looking for any investors?" I told him I wasn't, but I was curious and asked him what he had in mind. He said, "I know a couple of guys that might be interested in this." We followed through. And, that's how I got investors in my business I wasn't even looking for.

Tracie Hasse: That's Fantastic! Going back to the original guy that invited you up to the event, was he a friend of yours or a client?

Ron Nash: A friend. Well, let me back up. Some people found me on LinkedIn who were promoting a career event called *Career Reboot Camp.* They did it up in San Rafael, Marin County. They invited me to be one of their speakers. That's how we ended up becoming close friends. Whenever I go to Marin County, I stay at their home now. They found me on LinkedIn six or seven years ago and invited me to speak at a networking group, which lead them to creating a huge event around me.

Tracie Hasse: So that's what happened. Your story is so impactful on so many levels. You put yourself out there on LinkedIn first of all, right? I always tell people, "You've got to get yourself on LinkedIn. You never know who's looking for you, even while you are sleeping, right?"

Ron Nash: Absolutely!

Tracie Hasse: And then to hear these people found you on LinkedIn. You replied to their invitation and followed through. The thread of the magic that has happened, coupled with your passion, has been life changing for you. What I love about you is your desire to empower people because you do have a message that does make a difference in people's lives.

Ron Nash: Absolutely.

Tracie Hasse: And that is the bigger picture and what drove you to get up there to the event, right? It was not like, "Oh, I'm going to get paid a million dollars for this gig." It was more like, "I can't let my people down and I want to get up there and share this message to empower people to work their magic in the world."

Ron Nash: You are hitting on a good point. My fourth book is going to be about the power and magic of your "why." I have a very strong reason "why" I do anything.

Tracie Hasse: Speaking of books, congratulations on your newest book, *LinkedIn: The Power of Your Profile and Steps to Maximize Your Personal Brand*.

Ron Nash: Tracie, I'd like to share one final thought and probably one of the most important things that I can share. In my live events and in my online and printed publications I always address the power of your personal brand. Since we've officially entered the 21st Century, digital media has played an increasing role in our lives.

The appearance of social networks has given each person the ability to have a digital persona, and the thing I find that many people need more awareness of, is the fact that if you are online, people see you while you are sleeping.

Thus, if you are a business owner or aspiring one, job seeker or in transition, an executive, investor, veteran in transition, etc., your online profile needs to look the part of what you are aspiring to do or what you are currently doing - professionally.

In other words, you must look like the person who prepares for a business meeting, online and 24/7. This persona should also be adjusted at certain times, i.e. every 3-6 months, adding or adjusting something on your profile. This notifies your network that you are actively participating and creates profile views on LinkedIn.

I give a ton of strategies on building strong personal brand on LinkedIn, as well as, how to maximize it, in my new book, *LinkedIn: The Power of Your Profile and Steps to Maximize Your Personal Brand.*

I truly, truly appreciate you including me and interviewing me for this. I am excited for you. Let me know how I can help you.

Tracie Hasse: Infinite thank you's, Ron, for your time and for being such an inspiration to me! I am grateful to have you in my life.

I included this interview because it illustrates the power of networking and the opportunities it can create. Networking can be life changing.

Ch. 4 Recap: Proactive Prosperity

Thought Provoking Questions to Think About

- How are you going to *Go Big AND Stay Home*? What does that mean for you?
- Who are your online connections?
- Have you optimized your LinkedIn Profile so your target audience can find you?
- How could you use LinkedIn as your online marketing channel to leverage your network and resources?
- Are you using Facebook and Twitter to add friends, fans, and followers to your network?

Mindful Reflections

- A powerful network is one that helps you overcome challenges by connecting you to resources and people for collaboration to get things done.
- Try this strategy: Use Facebook and Twitter to expand your visibility and grow your contacts. Use LinkedIn to capitalize on your business connections.
- Use technology to leverage your strategic alliances and referral partners.

PART III:

PROACTIVE PROSPERITY

Chapter 5:
Referrals are Critical for Success

Growing your business through the power of referrals starts with you. Referrals help everyone. If you are a solo-entrepreneur, small business owner, sales professional or working for a large corporation, referrals make success even more fun and easy. Developing a robust sustainable referral system within your network requires a giving mindset versus a taking mindset in order for everyone to succeed and prosper. If you focus on how you can help others, eventually the domino effect will reward you in return, as referrals from grateful referral partners start flowing your way.

Your relationships with family, friends, employees, loyal clients, and potential clients are the core of your referral network. Once you get the hang of the referral game, it will come naturally and easily to you and your referral partners. You will all start working smarter not harder by leveraging each other's networks more effectively through the power of referrals. A momentum will build as you get into the "referral zone."

Referrals open doors to opportunities that create strategic alliances with other people and businesses in your network. These alliances have the potential to lead to lucrative business deals and the formation of powerful partnerships. Optimizing and leveraging your relationships keeps you top of mind in other people's networks so they are on the lookout for opportunities on your behalf.

If you want to change your life, job, or career, having a "Referral Mindset" can help you make those transitions smoother and easier. Mastering the art of connecting people through referrals helps you grow your network and your business.

You have a choice to live the life of your dreams or not. It takes courage, an open mind, being available to connect, and looking out for new opportunities that help you move forward in your career and life.

8 Reasons Why People are Dissatisfied in Their Jobs:

1. **They are not appreciated**

2. **They are not encouraged or empowered to seek advancement opportunities**

3. **Low self-worth**

4. **Lack of confidence in their abilities**

5. **Unaware of other possibilities and opportunities**

6. **People Pleasing; doing what someone else wants them to do**

7. **Resigned and stuck in a rut with no exit plan**

8. **Work and family life imbalances from working too much**

It's wonderful to be successful in a career or business, but not at the expense of living a well balanced and fulfilling life that you love living. Life is not meant to be all work and no play. Gain clarity about what you want out of life. Start asking yourself questions that cause you to take a deeper look at your life and career path. Here are a few to help you get started:

- **What is your definition of a great life?**
- **Do you envision yourself having your own business?**
- **Are you driven to make millions of dollars?**
- **What lifestyle do you aspire to live?**
- **What are you passionate about?**
- **How will you achieve your dream lifestyle and career?**

My incredible life coach, Bob, helped me gain clarity about living my life on purpose. He helped me see that I am either living with conscious choice and intention, or in an unconscious manner on autopilot.

I realized that in order for me to live my life consciously I have to be present.

Option 1: Be-Do-Have: The Conscious Way

Living my life consciously helps me move forward in life with less effort and more ease. It helps me plug into the positive flow of energy that attracts positive people and unexpected miracles to happen in my life.

1. It all starts with "Being" present and conscious in order to align with what you desire.

2. "Doing" starts with "Being." When you have the "Being" part down, it magnetizes good people, experiences, and opportunities into your life. The "Being" precedes the "Doing."

3. Appreciate what you "Have". An attitude of gratitude is the most powerful way to manifest your dreams.

Option 2. Do-Have-Be: The Unconscious Way

1. Trying to make things happen rather than letting things happen. "Doing" whatever it takes to force outcomes.

2. Trying to "Keep up with the Jones" and "Have" it all.

3. Surrender and give up as a last resort. "Being" resigned because you don't know what else to do.

The Unconscious Way requires more efforting than the Conscious Way. In the Unconscious Way, you come up against a lot of resistance by trying to make things happen, no matter what. Be aware that the more you resist, the more that thing persists. Right? By acknowledging and realizing your resistance, you are making peace with it by giving it space to just be. When you stop resisting and start accepting, life becomes more peaceful, pleasant, and easy.

Referrals are Critical for Success

The clearer you are about your dreams, the more the universe delivers on your behalf to bring your dreams to fulfillment. Resources can appear out of nowhere when you least expect them to give you the boost you need. Once you are conscious of where you want to go, take action, and start moving in that direction.

Consider the analogy of a car driving down a dark and windy road at night. The driver cannot see what's around the next curve, only what the head lights reveal in front of him. Thus it's an act of faith that he will arrive safely to a destination he cannot see. Very similarly, one must believe in his or her direction and have faith that, through consistent thought and action, their goal will be reached.

Try this simple fun exercise to expand your mind, creativity, and emotions. I learned this from Jean Houston, a brilliant thought leader, author, and creative genius:

1) Start by setting a timer for one-minute. Then shut your eyes. Imagine yourself traveling around the world.

2) Instant recall: Once the minute is up, stop and reflect on what that experience was like. Did it feel real? You just experienced a taste of traveling the world in your 'mind's eye.' The emotional energy of connecting to that experience can fuel the energy for you to actually have that experience in reality.

3) Now do this same exercise. Set the timer for one minute to visualize your dream life, career, or whatever you are trying to achieve.

Jean talks about warping space and time by doing this exercise. Try it for a couple of minutes each day. You have nothing to lose and everything to gain.

Referrals are the greatest compliment you can give someone. When you refer someone it means you trust and value that person and the product or service they provide so much that you are willing to put your reputation on the line to refer them to your family, friends, and clients.

11 Questions to Set Up Your Business for Success With Referrals:

1. How do you grow your business? How are referrals generated?

2. Are there other businesses that have a synergistic connection to yours? Would it be mutually beneficial to develop them as referral partners?

3. What is your business mission statement?

4. Is there an empowering philosophy of guiding principles for building your business?

5. Does your marketing message convey the greater purpose of your business and your uniqueness?

6. How does your business serve others?

7. Is your team of employees and affiliates aware of and in alignment with your mission statement?

8. Do you have a system in place to track your business referrals?

9. Where are your referrals coming from?

10. Who on your team is responsible for creating and generating referrals?

11. Are you thinking of others by referring them to opportunities that can help them get what they need?

When like-minded individuals do business together good things happen and a synergy is created that grows and builds momentum that's good for business. Referrals encourage and empower individuals to share their innate gifts and talents. That becomes the driving force for everyone's business growth and success. Tapping into this wellspring of synergies makes your company powerful and exciting to be a part of. You become a company people want to work with because they feel recognized and appreciated. When you refer business to other people in your network it is your way of showing your appreciation of them through your actions.

11 Hot Tips on How to Refer and Connect with People to Grow Business:

1. Determine who would be synergistic referral partners for you and your business.

2. Think about what businesses compliment your business by serving the same clients with related services to yours.

3. Write a list of the businesses and industries that are synergistic to your business.

4. Who are the people in your network that work in those businesses? Create a list of referral partner contacts in these related industries. Write down all their contact information.

5. Call the people on your list to schedule a time to meet and discuss the possibility of becoming referral partners. Create strategic alliances with key people in related companies to yours.

6. Send new referral partners a personalized note to connect on LinkedIn and Friend request on Facebook. Show them your intentions are sincere for creating a mutually beneficial referral partnership that will be good for their business as well as yours.

7. If you don't have a direct contact for a service you need, go to your network of people and find someone who does. Ask them for a referral.

8. Check out individuals on LinkedIn and Facebook by reviewing your "Shared Connections" to see how you are connected with them.

9. Once you find a "Shared Connection" for a service you need, send a note on LinkedIn or Facebook, and call your connection to request an introduction.

10. Leverage your network by asking for a warm introduction from someone you know that is connected with the person you would like to meet.

11. Increase your chances for successful connections with a combination of a phone call plus a text and/or email via LinkedIn, Facebook Personal Messaging, or traditional email.

I leverage my network through referral partnerships. Some of these partners include life coaches, branding and marketing experts, online reputation management companies, a literary agent and business model-licensing wizard. Each partner has helped me make career transitions, and launch my consulting business that I run from my home office, so I could Go Big AND Stay Home, while honoring my innate gifts and talents.

I refer clients to my Resources for their expertise and they refer clients to me for my expertise. We each take the time to understand each other's businesses and the type of clients that are a fit for each of us. We compliment, enhance, and prosper each other's businesses through our referral partnerships. Be mindful that potential partners are everywhere.

I marvel at the power of relationships. It is amazing to me to see where they started and what they have developed into today. A "Referral Mindset" is when you and your referral partners treat each other's businesses as if they were your own. There is reciprocity of give and take that contributes to everyone's success. Creating referral partnerships strengthens your relationships because you are investing in each other's business growth and success.

I have another story about my friend Barbi that illustrates this perfectly. Barbi introduced me to one of my incredible coaches Christopher, over 10 years ago. I started participating in his guided meditations that he led via a teleconference call. People from all over the world were on these inspiring calls. I resonated with Christopher and his work. Through these teleconference calls, I discovered that Christopher did individual life coaching sessions. I was ready for additional support, so I hired him as my life coach.

His divine coaching was the inspiration I needed to start up my consulting business. Our coaching sessions helped me discover my soul purpose and appreciate my natural talent for connecting people through the power of networking. Christopher understood and appreciated my gifts and talents so much that he invited me to join his team as the LinkedIn Strategist and Digital Marketing Consultant at Right Source Digital, Inc. A company he co-founded with Rewa, who was also a client of his. Right Source Digital, Inc. is an online digital marketing company that works to promote thought leaders and their businesses online. I never imagined that ten years later, I would be a key resource in one of Christopher's companies. I feel so blessed and grateful to be part of a team with such brilliant, wise, and business savvy individuals.

There was another opportunity where friends invited me to a networking event. At that event I met Rebecca, who owns a marketing and business coaching company for women entrepreneurs. Rebecca and I connected and were on the same wavelength. We saw an opportunity for working together since we had businesses that complemented each other. We scheduled a coffee date to get to know each other and our businesses better.

Rebecca suggested I check out a networking group she attended in Rancho Santa Fe called *Women's Wisdom*. Women's Wisdom has endured the test of time with the brilliant heart-centered leadership of Judy Ann and Ken D Foster.

After checking out Women's Wisdom online, I decided at the last minute to attend the monthly luncheon. It was one of the most well organized networking events I had ever attended. I was so impressed by the quality of women I met there. I have been attending their monthly luncheons ever since.

I met Ariela Wilcox the next month at Women's Wisdom. We clicked immediately. I was fascinated and curious about her profession as a Literary Agent. I wanted to find out how she helped people leverage their expertise and intellectual property by becoming published authors. So we met and I hired her to help me write my first book! Ariela has a unique approach. She is the only Literary Agent in the United States who uses her 40 years of business experience to coach her clients to write a book in only 6 weeks. It has been an extraordinary growth experience that has empowered me professionally and personally. She showed me that I had something of value to say and share. So here I am writing this book.

Had I not gone to that one instrumental networking event and followed up with Rebecca, I wouldn't have met Ariela, the person who encouraged and coached me to share my expertise by writing a book. Now that is networking synergy!

There have been times while writing this book that I had no idea what to write. So I would turn to my partner Reed and Ariela to remind me of how important the book was. They held the vision for me and encouraged me on my book writing journey. Then there's incredible Writing Diva Deb who came along in the perfect time to polish up my story with her editing and writing expertise. I am so grateful for their love, support, and belief in me. I could not have done it without them!

The greatest gifts that I treasure are business referrals. When I receive a call from a person who has been referred to me, I stand up and do the happy dance! Don't you just love getting referrals? It makes me so happy that someone valued me and my expertise enough to refer someone to me. When someone refers me business it is because they trust me. They also save the person they referred a lot of time and frustration trying to find what they need through trial and error and doing a bunch of research.

Rebecca had been helping her client Valerie with her branding and marketing message. She introduced me to Valerie at Women's Wisdom one day. Valerie hired me to help her set up her LinkedIn account. During our LinkedIn strategy session, we were able to use all the content she created with Rebecca to market her brand through her LinkedIn profile.

Valerie was excited about the synergy of how Rebecca's expertise and mine complemented each other to help her get what she needed. It was a good investment in her business. She appreciated the clarity she gained to market her business more effectively from working with each of us. She became a happy client and great referral partner for both Rebecca and me.

Rebecca also was delighted to receive a referral check and thank you note from me for referring Valerie. I believe it is important to nurture referral partnerships by showing my appreciation in a personal way. I am a fan of the old-fashioned, almost extinct, practice of sending hand-written *Thank You* notes that I slip my referral checks into. People really appreciate thoughtful little acts of kindness with a personal touch. Try it sometime and see what happens. You may be pleasantly surprised.

**Being a "Resource" is empowering and fun.
Being "Resourceful" makes you a
valuable asset to your network.**

Is the light bulb going on for you yet, about all the opportunities being a referral resource can open up for you and your business?

What do I mean by resource? When you refer people, you become a resource or rather the source of resources, by connecting people to other people who can help them get what they need. Are you the person that people call because you are in the know and well connected with resources they need?

Being resourceful starts with taking the time to get to know the people you consider your core circle of influence. They are in your Success Circles. Take the time to find out more about them, their lives, and their businesses by asking them questions. Schedule quality time to learn more about the people in your referral network. It is a good investment of your time that will pay off. Find out how you can be a resource for them.

For example, if you are a Realtor, synergistic referral sources for you would be Estate and Trust Attorneys, Certified Public Accountants (CPAs), financial industry experts, general contractors, title and escrow reps, escrow officers, mortgage bankers, and home inspectors, because you all serve the same clients in different ways that complement each other. These related businesses can become strategic alliances in which you build a referral pipeline that is mutually beneficial for all your businesses and your clients as well. Everyone wins! The first step is to schedule a time to meet them and discuss the possibility of becoming referral partners who prosper together.

When you connect with people and show them your sincere interest in helping or serving them, you build trust.

Get to know people. Show them you are interested in them and their lives, businesses, and concerns. Ask questions to find out more about them. What are the missing links in their lives personally or professionally? What if their enthusiasm for life was reignited as a result of a resource you provided to them? Are they looking to hire a key employee for their business? Are they in need of strategic alliances to help them expand their businesses? Be that person that takes the conversation to the next level. Ask questions that help you understand them, so you can better serve them. At the very least, you will leave a good impression as someone who is sincere, trustworthy, and cares. They will appreciate you for your interest in them. And most likely, you will be top of mind when they have a referral.

Referrals work both ways. Think of the people around you and how to help them solve their problems by referring a resource to them. It is a fun and lucrative way to help others and make some money while you're at it!

Referrals have given me a wonderful business, life-long friendships, and extraordinary opportunities to grow and prosper. Referrals are an integral part of my life!

It's been so much fun to watch the power of what a referral can do. I met Ariela, a literary agent, through a referral to an event. I was thrilled when I was able to give her this referral:

The Referral

- I met my friend Michele when we worked for Tony Robbins. She is a *Results Coaching Consultant*. She also does personal coaching. Michele is a single-mom raising three small children.

The Problem

- She was on call and worked long hours for her coaching job. She wanted to spend more quality time with her family without sacrificing income.

The Solution

- Find a way to leverage her expertise so she wasn't trading time for dollars. How could she work smarter not harder and make money while she spent time with her family?
- I referred Michele to Ariela Wilcox, of The Wilcox Agency in Del Mar, because Ariela offers a unique service that could help Michele get out of the rat race she was trapped in.
- Ariela Wilcox is the only Literary Agent in the United States who teaches people how to license their business

model and make money from their present business or service. Ariela has also designed a lucrative and sustainable "Coaching Network" Signature Program with the potential to generate over $240,000 in annual revenue with 200 or less coaches in the network. The best part of this business model is that you would only spend *one day per month* to coach, mentor, teach, talk with and answer questions, etc. The *rest of the month you would be free* to do other things like speaking at events, have private clients or patients, travel or do fun things! The "Coaching Network" has a unique built in distribution system that helps coaches, speakers, trainers, and consultants promote their books and products through the network.

- It's perfect for Doctors, Coaches, Trainers, Consultants, Alternative Doctors or any professional who 1.) has a System, Methods, Medical Or Psychological Protocols and 2.) procedures that they want to share with many more people than they could reach with their expertise.

- With the power of leverage and duplication a person who had a "Coaching Network" of their own will have a sustainable business model that protects their intellectual property, enables them to build wealth, and helps people have their own business.

- Michelle was able to leverage her expertise as a coach using Ariela's "Coaching Network" Signature Program. Thanks to Ariela and the power of a good referral, Michele is on her way to increasing her income to ultimately spend more time with her children.

Referrals are Critical for Success

Because I referred Michele to Ariela, she received a new client. Michele was open to Ariela's solution to solve her problem. And, Ariela paid me a referral fee for doing something I would have done for free that I love to do. I got to support two incredible people in my life that created a trifecta 'win-win-win' for all of us! That's how referral marketing works!

It is important to make sure it is a good fit with a potential referral partner. Prequalify them by asking questions that help you determine if they will be a good referral partner for you.

Prequalify Potential Referral Partners with these Questions:

1. What is your business specialty?

2. Who are your target clients?

3. Is there synergy between our businesses that makes sense for us to refer clients to each other?

4. How do you work with clients; one-on-one, groups, workshops, or webinars?

5. What geographic region do you work in?

6. Review and sign a Referral Partnership Agreement, to form a simple legal contract that clearly states the terms of the partnership and the amounts of the referral fees. If someone isn't willing to sign this agreement then question their motives and run in the other direction.

The key to referral relationships is that they are mutually beneficial for all parties involved. If you are the only person engaging and trying to help prosper another without anything in return that is a one-sided relationship you should end. Do not waste your time with takers. Actions speak louder than words. Watch what people do, rather than listening to promises that never lead to referrals from them. Are both parties making efforts to follow-up with each other and do the things they said they would do? Be discerning. Observe. If people say one thing and their actions aren't consistent with their words. Believe their actions, not their words.

Referral magic happens when all parties involved open their hearts and have the attitude of being there for each other. Take the initiative to engage and dig deeper with individuals by asking insightful questions about their business and how you could be a resource for them. Share what you are doing, what you are in need of, and your challenges in your business. Connect and communicate to find out how you can mutually benefit each other. You never know who they may have in their network that might be a key resource for your business growth. How are you able to help them with what you do and with the expertise of the people in your network?

Be generous. Share your wealth of knowledge and how your life has been enhanced by a person, service, or product. This is how businesses thrive and grow through the power of referrals.

One of my favorite things to do is write referral checks to the people that have referred clients to me. I have received referrals from clients, people who I have referral partnerships with, companies I have strategic alliances with, and of course from the people in my success circles. People refer me business because they are confident that I am going to take care of their client or friend and deliver results that help them. Receiving referrals is a sign of success. Referrals are proof that you are providing a quality product or service that is enhancing people's lives. People don't give referrals to businesses that don't deliver. Referrals are your reward for exceeding expectations by serving others.

In today's fast-paced world of business who you know matters. Building a strong network of relationships is essential to gain a competitive edge that opens doors to opportunity. LinkedIn and Facebook are key social networks that enable you to harness the power of technology to expand your network exponentially.

Helping others succeed is the best and fastest way to grow a business and prosper in life. Take the spotlight off of yourself and put it on the people in your life. Focus on how you can help others by referring them to a resource or service that can help them.

A referral mindset is a success mindset because referrals are good for business. Be a referral magnet that spreads success and prosperity, and attracts it too.

The most effective way to become a master at referrals is to be yourself and connect with an open heart. Let people in. Let them see who you really are. Be open, transparent, and vulnerable. People will fall in love with you and trust you if you do.

When you take the risk to be vulnerable you make it safe for others to open up and be vulnerable too. This takes courage. It requires you to be your authentic genuine self. This makes others feel safe with you and builds trust.

Honor yourself and others by connecting with your heart through the power of authenticity? Try it out by taking small steps. Share something real about yourself with someone. It doesn't have to be a deep dark secret, just something they don't know about you personally. It could be something as heartwarming as telling them how much you love your dog. Experiment and see how it impacts your life. You will never know unless you try.

Success Circles consist of the people closest to you that you feel safe to be your authentic self with. They are your referral teams who know you well both online and offline. Success Circles build confidence because you are part of a supportive community with a shared vision to connect and collaborate for the benefit of everyone. There is a ripple effect that helps you grow your business by expanding your network. Success Circles provide camaraderie, accountability, and encouragement, as you help each other reach greater business success.

Ch. 5 Recap: Proactive Prosperity

Thought Provoking Questions to Think About

- How are you going to *Go Big AND Stay Home*? What does that mean for you?
- Are you leveraging social media channels to expand your exposure online?
- Are you dissatisfied with your job? Are you taking actions to make a change?
- Are you proactive in creating prosperity for yourself and others through the power of networking and referrals?
- What actions can you take today to grow and build your business by referring?

Mindful Reflections

- Expand your business through the power of referrals. It starts with you helping someone with a referral.
- Being a "Resource" is empowering and fun. Being "Resourceful" makes you a valuable asset to your network.
- Technology makes it possible for us to expand our reach globally and build connections personally and professionally.
- You have a choice. Shift your energy to empower your life. Choose whether you want to live a mindful, conscious life, or an unconscious one.

PART IV:

SUCCESSFUL REFERRAL-BASED BUSINESS MODELS

Chapter 6:
Refer and Create Your Road to Riches

Throughout my life I have enjoyed building relationships, working, and generating cash flow, to empower myself, and others. I had a vision of investing my time in a business that I believe in, a business that has my best interests at heart, and especially one that I am passionate about. A business that resonates with my values, and benefits me and everyone it touches. One that I could do part-time or full-time, in-person or online. A business where I have the freedom and flexibility to connect with people around the world.

Evaluating business opportunities requires keen selectivity, in order to determine if it is a good opportunity or an illegal pyramid, also known as a "Ponzi" scheme. Experience and maturity have taught me discernment. If a business opportunity sounds too good to be true most likely it is. Proceed with caution.

- Do you have a method or system for evaluating opportunities?
- How do you know what to look for in a business?

- Is there transparency?
- Is it congruent with your values, integrity, and ethics to be involved with this business or industry?
- Do you trust and believe in the person who referred you?
- Do you use the products or service?

In my quest to find the right business opportunity that resonated with me, I discovered the **Direct to Consumer Marketing/ Manufacturing business model.** The marketing power and competitive advantage of this particular business model is because the "middle-man" is eliminated. It is an efficient, cost effective way to deliver high quality products from the manufacturer directly to the consumer. **Direct to Consumer** is a brilliant business model because it keeps marketing costs low and product value high.

Did you know that manufacturing companies spend more money marketing their products than they do on manufacturing them? For example, the average traditional manufacturing company spends approximately $63 out of every $100 on everything but the product. That means only $37, out of $100 is spent on creating the product. Where does all the other money go? That $63 pays for all the other operating and marketing costs. It pays for the "middle-man" costs.

Who is the "middle-man" and why is he being paid so much? "Middle-man" costs include:
- Outsourcing to contractors, vendors, and consultants
- Distribution and storage of products
- Marketing and advertising

- Paying for endorsements from super models, actors, and athletes
- Competitive rates for the best product placement in retail stores
- Leasing retail store space

The **Direct to Consumer** business model eliminates the middle-man costs and invests a significant amount of that $100 (from the previous example) in creating high quality products that are delivered directly to consumers at affordable prices.

The brilliance of this business model is that the company's loyal customers, who choose to be marketing executives educating on behalf of the company, do the marketing and advertising for them through word of mouth referral marketing. Happy, loyal customers that are compensated with referral checks, provide lots of referrals.

The huge opportunity here is in giving individuals a way to build their own business, at their own pace, whether they are currently employed or not. People have the potential to add income with a choice to work their business on their terms, either part time or full time. **Direct to Consumer Marketing** provides business owners a way to build residual income and keep their marketing costs low.

Several years ago, I had complications from back surgery that prevented me from working for several months. I was grateful I was working for a company that valued me as an employee and kept my job waiting for me until I recovered. But that is the exception rather than the norm. Most people aren't that lucky. That's why it's important to be prepared with a back-up plan when an unexpected set back occurs.

I believe everything happens for a reason, especially when I'm going through difficult experiences. It helps me get through them knowing there will be some kind of miracle or blessing on the other side of the difficulty. During my post operation recovery, I had a lot of time to think about and reflect on my life. I realized how quickly the security of a corporate job could be taken away. I felt very vulnerable and resolved to do something about it.

I had been in corporate America my entire career and was blessed to work with incredible people at amazing companies. Every once in a while though, the thought would creep into my head. *What is my back-up plan if this doesn't work? What would I do if I wasn't working in corporate America? What are my options for generating revenue beyond my salary?*

When I started thinking about having my own business without huge start-up costs that are typically required, I asked, "What are my options?" What is the leverage afforded by being a marketing representative educating for a Direct to Consumer company? I liked the idea of having a business where I have a choice to work part-time or full-time, with a solid foundation representing a top-notch, noble company. I started to search for my back-up plan to secure my financial future.

Saving and investing for retirement is a great plan, but how do you guarantee an income stream once you are no longer in the traditional job market?

What do you think of when you hear the word retirement? Does it empower you or fill you with dread? For me, retirement is about possibilities. When will I retire? Why would I retire if I am passionate about what I am doing, helping people with my divine gifts through my work? I see myself doing what I love as long as I am able to.

I understand the importance of preparing financially for retirement. I also see the beauty of living life fully in the now. There is no guarantee I will live a long life into old age. It is important to prepare for the unexpected with a back-up plan that provides multiple revenue sources.

My Grandma and Grandpa had always planned on traveling around the world when they retired. They dreamed of the great adventures and fun they would have traveling together. They never got to fulfill their retirement dreams. Over the course of ten years prior to retirement, my Grandpa had five heart attacks.

Watching what happened with my grandparents, when they lost their chance to enjoy retirement, lit a fire of desire in me to travel and enjoy life while I am still healthy, happy, and able. So I travel whenever I get the chance. Life is uncertain. Don't wait until retirement to start living. There are no guarantees. Take that dream trip while you still can. Don't wait.

I have lost too many people I love too soon. Their deaths inspired me to live my life fully and seize the moment to travel every chance I get. My Dad's father had a massive heart attack at forty-five years of age and died on the farm while working. My brother Todd was tragically killed when he was hit by a car at the age of twenty-nine. I watched Reed's dad struggle with illness over the course of many years. My Mom had pulmonary fibrosis for the last fourteen years of her life. Their deaths instilled an urgency in me to live life to the fullest and take chances and risks to *Go Big AND Stay Home* by following my heart.

I've enjoyed many travel adventures that have enriched my life tremendously. My brother Todd and I went backpacking through Western Europe for a month. I got to go on an African Safari and white water rafting down the Zambezi in class five rapids with two of my best girlfriends, Suzanne and Jeannette. At the turn of the century, I cheered in the New Year in Spain with my boyfriend Michael and toured the country for a whole month with a group of friends. I've had fun exploring Mexico and Hawaii. Reed and I spent a month traveling through Argentina from Buenos Aires to the southwest region along the Chilean border to the southern tip of Argentina, Ushuaia, where people come from all over the world to see the glaciers.

I've enjoyed traveling throughout the United States and Canada for business and fun too. I had a blast living with my Mom in Arlington, Virginia during one of my summer breaks from college. At that time she worked for our dear family friend, Senator Alan Simpson of Wyoming. We had fun touring Washington D.C. and the North Eastern part of the United States.

When I reflect on these amazing adventures I have experienced in my life, I realize that if I had spent too much time thinking about how everything was going to work out financially, I may not have gone big but instead stayed home. I had a bigger purpose and desire that drove me to take these trips, knowing all would work out in the end. Most importantly, I was willing to take the risk.

Many years ago, Barbi shared with me, "Tracie, the greater the risk, the greater the reward!" That's when I moved to San Diego, which has turned out to be my heaven on earth for me. I took a risk to Go Big AND find a new home to live in where my heart is happiest!

**What's your back-up plan for retirement
to *Go Big AND Stay Home*?
How can you plan and prepare for the
future while living your life fully now?
It's never too late to start saving and
investing in your dream life.**

Before you embark on a business with the freedom of a home office, see if the company you'd be representing is all it is hyped up to be. A lot of business owners avoid this crucial process. How can you fix something if you don't know what's broken? How can you capitalize on and duplicate what's working if you don't know what that is? Be diligent. Success starts with a **Strategic Business Evaluation**. Evaluate the key metrics closely in order to better forecast your success.

Make a decision you are passionate about and committed to investing your time in. An educated and empowered decision moves you forward positioned with the confidence you need to build your business. People will sense and respond to this confidence in an unspoken way. Are you ready to put your reputation on the line and represent the company? When the key metrics are met, your efforts will be rewarded.

I made many mistakes and lost a lot of money trying different businesses part-time in network marketing, multi-level marketing, and pyramid schemes that I didn't know were pyramid schemes until too late. Many promoters and executives of these types of companies are only interested in hyping up a company, getting in first, making the most money before the company disappears because it was not a sustainable business model. Many of these companies, but not all of them, are often shut down by one of the Attorneys General of a particular state for illegal business practices. So this is another reason to do due diligence.

I got caught up in the hype and didn't do enough research and due diligence before jumping in. I learned what not to do from my mistakes and losses. Now I educate and empower my clients to adapt systems and practices that will save them time and money from making the same costly mistakes I did and be profitable from the start. Your goodwill and credibility are critical elements to success and tough to regain once lost.

When somebody buys a traditional business or franchise it's a relatively straight-forward process consisting of approximately three steps:

1. Evaluate the Business opportunity via a Business Broker

2. Review Company, Sales and Tax Returns

3. Make a decision to purchase company by opening Escrow to formalize the deal over the course of 30+days, then close escrow.

But, with Direct to Consumer, Network Marketing, and Distribution Opportunities, a different criteria is in play. Ask a few more questions because most companies don't have this material available for your review. If you're looking at a private company, they don't have to disclose any of this information. So ask the person introducing you to an opportunity some of these questions. You'll look really smart and it's in your best interest.

A public company answers all of these questions. Here's a different way of evaluating a business or business opportunity.

I created a **Strategic Business Evaluation Checklist** of key metrics to review when you are considering business opportunities with the luxury and freedom of working from your home office. Look at business trends and the stats backing them.

**Business Wisdom 101: Don't start any
business until you have done
your due diligence. Use the Strategic
Business Evaluation Checklist
to help you evaluate the strengths
and weaknesses of business
opportunities before making any commitments.**

Strategic Business Evaluation Checklist

1. Key Business Metrics & Financial Wellness:
- Gather and Review Business Reports and History: How many years have they been in business? What is the company's legal track record? Is the company in any lawsuits now or have they been in the past?
- Does the company have outstanding debt or are they operating debt-free?
- Is company positioned for future long-term growth? Is it a recession proof business?

- Are they ethical and built on solid principles? Does it support your values?
- Think Retirement: Is this opportunity going to provide a reliable source of income? Does this business offer real leverage?
- Is there a cap on your earnings? Can you earn residual income?
- Is the business model competitive or one-sided in favor of the company only? Are they interested in spreading good will by sharing their good fortune with all involved?
- Does the business model empower financial prosperity for employees, employers, and marketing representatives?
- Is the leadership team comprised of experienced experts in the given industry? What is their background, education, and training? Do they have a solid vision and proven mission statement that they lead from?
- What is the customer/ referral partner ratio? For example, is it 75% customers to 25% business referral partners? This is a safe margin of error and a solid business. If the ratio is the reverse, 75% referral partners, and 25% customers, it's unlikely this business will last.
- What is the customer re-order and retention rate? What is the customer attrition rate?
- Does the company manufacture their own products? Is the company in control of its supply chain? Do they own their supply chain?

2. Market Positioning & Competitive Advantage:

- What percentage of the population is your target market?
- Does the company continue to expand growth based on trends in the marketplace?
- Does the company have a nimble and efficient business model relative to its competitors?
- Do they offer superior quality products compared to their competitors? Do patents, trademarks, or copyrights protect their products? Are their products made in the USA or globally?
- Is there a budget for new product development? Do the products have a competitive advantage and longevity?
- What is their business model? Does Customer Satisfaction drive the business model? Do customers receive valuable Perks and Benefits?
- Is their product a one-time only purchase or are there products customers reorder on a regular basis? Does their product require a complex sales cycle with multiple presentations or is it a point of sale process?
- Do customers have a built in business opportunity by being a loyal customer OR is starting a business an additional significant investment/cost for all the business tools and trainings?
- Does their marketing message educate and empower prospects to make buying decisions that convert them into customers?

3. Industry Practices: Direct to Consumer Marketing, Network Marketing, Distributorships, or other Opportunities to Represent a Company:

- Do you understand the difference between these common business models and the opportunity being presented to you? The business models noted are common business models for marketing and selling a product or service.
- Do you understand the compensation plan?
- Are you required to buy inventory to enhance your pay structure?
- Are the majority of people customers, approximately 65%, and the other 35% business builders? If yes, then your odds for success increase having a sustainable business model based on loyal clients. This is an indication of a healthy business and far from a pyramid scheme.
- Are you a distributor? Is product retailing a part of the business model?
- Are you selling to consumers or educating consumers so they can buy directly from the company?
- Is the compensation plan transparent or complicated and difficult to understand? Is there a cap on your income?
- Does this business provide an opportunity to earn residual or referral income?
- In reference to estate planning, are you able to transfer your revenue from your business to your family?
- What is the lost opportunity cost if you don't get involved in the business?
- What type of training, business systems, and customer support do you have as a marketing representative?

Build a reliable, residual income with a company that is mission driven and offers a future that enables you to thrive, succeed, and enjoy retirement.

Be on the lookout for opportunities. Look for trends in up and coming industries and opportunities that offer commissions, bonuses, and other incentives to increase your income. Find a company that has consistent annual growth and is innovative and expanding their product line in an evolving market. What is their schedule to take a new product to market? Do they have an efficient system for bringing new products to market in order to capitalize on market trends and demands?

Do the research required to find the business that is right for you. Use my *Strategic Business Evaluation Checklist* to evaluate new business opportunities. Talk to people who have been in the business you are checking out. Meet industry leaders. Visit the corporate office to see what the vibe is like. Talk to people throughout the company at all levels to get a feel for their company culture. Invest the time to find out if this is a business you could thrive and succeed in.

Once you have chosen the right business for you let your network of people know about it so they can support you and get involved in the new opportunity too. They can support your success and benefit from it too. Don't be shy about getting the support you need through networking. It's good for business and your network too.

Networking is happening all around us whether we are conscious of it or not. Is your "net" "working"? Are you consciously and deliberately making connections to build a strong network of resources that you can use to help people and grow your business. Whenever you are engaged in a conversation with someone new, you are networking. Whenever you ask someone what they do, you are networking. Whenever you ask for help or refer someone to a resource that helps them, you are networking. People network and don't even realize they are doing it, because it comes so naturally when human beings come together in community to connect and get to know each other. Most people are natural networkers and don't even realize it.

Did you know that you are networking when:

- **You take your kids to the park and meet someone who tells you about a new product you try that becomes the miracle remedy for your child's eczema or asthma.**
- **You get together with your friends to try out a new restaurant that one of your friends discovered.**
- **You tell your Dad about a natural wellness supplement that helps him reduce his need for prescription drugs and improves his vitality and zest for life.**
- **Your dear friend shares her experience of how she lost 10 pounds and is sleeping better. You want to know how she did it, right?**
- **You're at a training workshop learning about new resources to improve your business from the speaker and through people you're networking with at the event.**

- You go to happy hour with friends to catch up and share the latest and greatest with each other.
- You take a romantic trip with the love of your life and discover the most spectacular get-a-way and share it with everyone you know when you return.
- You refer a friend in need to a new opportunity.
- When people ask you, "Where did you get your hair styled?" you refer them to your stylist.
- You call friends to ask them if they know of a great house cleaner.
- Your realtor gets ready to list your house and she has a referral network of contractors to help you prepare your house to sell.
- You ask your friends who they use for their life, medical, and car insurance.

People engage in conversation with people they care about. That is the start of networking. The magic of networking is simple but profound. It's when two or more people connect, communicate, and refer resources to each other that enhance their quality of lives and help them succeed. Connecting with people and sharing products and services that can benefit them is networking.

A close friend introduced me to the **Direct to Consumer Marketing** business model and explained how you're able to generate residual income through referrals. Referring to a Direct to Consumer Company enables you to build income for your retirement. You build your business by networking and creating referral partners. How many companies have sent you checks for referring people to their products or services?

After all my years in corporate America, not one of those companies mailed me monthly checks after I left for building their business when I was an employee. Imagine opening your mailbox and receiving a bonus check from a company you used to work for? Included in the check is a Thank you note that reads, "Thank You for all your efforts for all those years. We couldn't have done it without your help!"

Direct to Consumer Marketing companies enable more people to realize their dream of owning their own business, so they have more freedom and time with their families while building a secure future.

Here are a few success stories of people I know who went for it to, *Go Big AND Stay Home.* They found a company that has been life changing for them. It has given them the freedom to own their own business yet be supported by a world class company and run their business with an office at home, and the flexibility of creating their own schedule.

Angie's Story:

"I'm a mom with three sons and…I was a mortgage broker. My partners and I were the #1 originating team in San Diego County with a large bank, but when the economy pulled the rug out from underneath us in 2008, I wasn't even making enough to cover my draw. My husband was the president of a company that required him to travel five days a week. We agreed that it was best for me to go back to being a "stay at home mom" again…and ride out the recession – fully intending to come back to the mortgage industry. That's all great in theory until I had to send my oldest son to college. I had promised him that if he worked hard and had the grades to get into a good university that we will do everything we could to be able to pay for him to go there.

So, I was looking around for different opportunities and options to be able to replace my six-figure income in the mortgage industry, but still be able to "be a mom". I did a lot of research. A friend introduced me to a direct to consumer manufacturing company. I was impressed by the company and their approach. The people were professional, well-educated and from a variety of different backgrounds. There were realtors, doctors, and teachers. I saw how well they were doing and how happy they were. I liked how they worked as a team. I decided to go for it!

Sometimes I work two hours a day. Other times I work ten hours a day. I can schedule my work around my family's schedule, and that's a blessing to me. This company has changed my life because it has allowed me to own my own business, run it from my home office, and still be able to be at home with my boys. We have been able to secure a financial future and I get to be a total mom at the same time."

Angie isn't the only one who made her dream of having her own business with a home office a reality. Dr. Barbara, a successful surgeon, was ready for a change too.

Dr. Barbara's Story

"I attended medical school for four years at The Mayo Clinic in Rochester, Minnesota. Subsequent to that, I completed my 5-year general surgery residency at Loma Linda University Medical Center. I then served in the U.S. Navy as a general/trauma surgeon after 9/11 in 2001 and very much enjoyed my surgical career. I eventually opened my own private practice in Orange County, California, upon completing my plastics and reconstructive residency at Vanderbilt University Medical Center.

When I was introduced to a company with a solid foundation for income generation to include residual income and also the ability to create time freedom, I was very intrigued but wasn't really sure if it would work for me. Working 85, 97, sometimes more than 100 hours per week with a crazy call schedule did not allow for many new ventures. And I was already spending a tremendous amount of time away from my family. But I weighed my options and my aspirations and courageously dove into making a change and a difference in not only my life but also others. I met a lot of people like me, who were successful, educated, hard workers who wanted a more balanced lifestyle without sacrificing their financial security.

My life today is very different compared to six years ago. I have actually been able to take Christmas vacations, which I had not done during my entire surgical career. I am able to make it to all the important events in my family's lives, and family dinners, too. I can take time off and arrange my schedule for out of town guests who want to visit. Time also exists for other endeavors that I have always dreamt of pursuing.

My decision and my perseverance have changed my life. I see my family and spend time with my husband now. I'm not scared about losing my marriage or not being there for my aging parents when they need me. I know that I can actually take time off for travel to take care of them or to see them when I need to. I am enveloped in hope. I know that sounds strange coming from a surgeon. A traditional surgical practice is a fantastic career and I love to operate. But now I have my own business that allows me to spend quality time with those that I love, while also making a great income and helping others to do the same. Now my life overflows with relationships, building others up and paying it forward, enjoying friends and family, and not working 24/7 but empowering others in their own abilities, health, and providing hope where it had been abandoned."

Dr. Barbara was able to successfully launch her business and still have time for surgery. Most importantly, her new business allows her to spend more time with family and friends.

Kara already had a real estate business but needed more security. She needed to diversify to generate revenue she could count on.

Kara's Story

"We moved to San Diego from the Bay Area. I decided I wanted a change so I got my real estate license. I've been a real estate broker for over 15 years. In real estate, it is pretty simple; if I'm not working, I'm not earning money. My husband and I were used to living on commissions and not receiving regular monthly paychecks. Our real estate business was flourishing. We were doing well. I didn't think I could find anything better to replace that. To be honest, I never thought that there was something else out there that could make me the kind of money my real estate business did. I can't imagine working for someone else. I'm virtually unemployable, because I've been a business owner for so long; nobody wants to hire someone who is so independent.

Then my friend introduced me to a company (Direct to Consumer Marketing Company) that actually became the perfect opportunity for me because I realized that I could do it alongside my real estate business. I didn't have to give up all the sweat equity in my real estate business. I am proud to say it evolved into a business that provides a six-figure income for me now."

Kara didn't give up her Real Estate business with her husband. She's thrilled to be making a 6-figure income in addition to her real estate business. Most importantly she appreciates the quality time with her husband and daughter.

If a mortgage broker, doctor, and realtor can find freedom to live the good life you can too!

The point of sharing these stories is to showcase successful business women who discovered a way to build a business from home, or wherever they are in the world, with a work schedule suited to their lifestyle. They were open to possibilities and discovered a business that leverages networking, the Internet, and referrals for success. Explore and be open to options to integrate a new opportunity into your life, either part-time or full-time.

Recently I heard a company advertisement on the radio that went something like this: "Hey we're selling ice cream shop franchise opportunities. We're accepting applications and a $10,000 deposit!" That's just the franchise fee.

Find a company like these women have, that doesn't include any of the traditional start-up costs: inventory, leasing a space, hiring employees, and the list goes on. Let's face it buying any business franchise requires a hefty investment that is not feasible for most people. The good news is there are other solid opportunities to choose from.

Most importantly represent a noble and respectable company that you are proud to educate and refer to people you care about.

Are you ready to build the life of your dreams? What do you have to lose?

- Take control of your future now. Start with baby steps to put your dreams in motion. Write them down. Make a phone call. Make a commitment to yourself. Take one step every day to honor your dreams.
- Be your biggest fan.
- Commit to learning the skills and beating the odds through personal development. Knowledge is power and that can never be taken away from you. This will help you in every aspect of your life from building confidence to making money.
- Team up with others who complement your skillset and help put your business in motion. Camaraderie and accountability bring joy and productivity to whatever you do.
- Why is it most people fail? ... They stop trying. So don't stop trying.

Ch. 6 Recap: Proactive Prosperity

Thought Provoking Questions to Think About

- How are you going to *Go Big AND Stay Home*? What does that mean for you?
- Is your "net" working?
- Are you looking for the next opportunity, or the last opportunity to save and invest for your retirement?
- How can you stop trading time for dollars and leverage your network to build a business with a residual monthly income?

Mindful Reflections

- Direct to Consumer Marketing/Manufacturing business model eliminates the "middle-man" by delivering high quality products at wholesale prices directly to the consumer, while also creating residual income for people looking for opportunities.
- Direct to Consumer Referral Businesses rely on social networking and word-of-mouth referrals to grow, succeed, and prosper.
- Business Wisdom 101: Use my Strategic Business Evaluation Checklist to evaluate business opportunities.
- Research opportunities until you find the business model that suits you and that you are passionate about.

PART V:

GO BIG AND STAY HOME

Chapter 7:

Inspiration & Actions for Going Big AND Staying Home

Shhh … take a moment to pause and take a few deep breaths to quiet your mind and relax your body. You may even want to set a timer for three minutes. You deserve this time for yourself. Listen to yourself breathing. Feel your heart beat. That's the miracle of life. After three minutes, take note of how you are feeling. How is your energy level? Do you find yourself more present in this moment? Great! I just did the same thing to prepare to write this last chapter.

Taking a few minutes for yourself every day is a simple way to create space for greater inspiration, patience, joy, and success in your daily life.

People are so busy rushing through life trying to meet their daily demands on their time. Life is full of distractions that detour us in many directions. Living an intentional and committed life requires focus and dedication to what you are trying to achieve. Take some time out to just "be" instead of always doing. It will help you gain clarity on what's important to you and how to prioritize your life.

Ask yourself a few simple questions to tune in to yourself right now:

- **How do you feel on a scale of 1 = lousy to 10 = Super?**
- **What thoughts are pulling on your attention?**
- **Do you believe there should be more to life?**
- **Are you feeling overwhelmed?**
- **What inspires you?**
- **Do you love what you do?**
- **Do your accomplishments get recognized at work?**
- **Do you respect the people you work with?**
- **Do you feel they respect you?**
- **Do you create your work schedule or does someone else?**
- **Are you passionate about the company you're working with whether it is your company or someone else's?**
- **Are you happy in your job?**
- **Are you hoping for a pay raise?**
- **Have you ever dreamed of having your own business to build, grow, and prosper from?**
- **Are you earning residual income?**
- **Do you have enough free time to play, travel, and spend time with loved ones?**
- **Do you have a plan for your retirement?**
- **Is your retirement going according to plan?**

Did those questions leave you wondering what's next for you and your life? I asked myself these questions when I was doing some soul searching. It is my intention to build a bridge for you to get from where you are now to where you would like to be in your life, by providing resources for you. It starts with desire. Are you ready to take your life to the next level?

Start by spending time creating a "vision" for your life. A vision is essential because it becomes your roadmap to achieving your dreams. Would you go on a road trip to a place you have never been without a map? Without a map, you most likely will not arrive at your destination. Your odds of arriving at your destination in a timely manner increase significantly with a map.

Do you feel you are on the brink of something great? Are you struggling to make it happen? Let your vision guide you to gain clarity on your goals. It starts with your vision which drives your actions. Your vision is your strategic roadmap to success. If you are wondering how to create your life vision, I have a resource for you.

Jeffery Rogers has been a friend of mine since childhood. He has been empowering people and inspiring audiences for over 20 years. Through his company, BrainStormSuccess.com, he helps people discover, define, and clarify the vision for their lives with his *Magnitude Vision Course Coaching Program - Finally Achieve an Extraordinary Life of Clarity, Confidence, and Purpose.*

Words of Wisdom from Jeffery Rogers:

"When you create a clear, detailed vision of your life, you make serious decisions about the direction of your life and solutions to the challenges that keep

you from creating the life you desire become obvious. They were there all the time. It was your lack of clarity that kept you from seeing and utilizing them to your advantage. Once those resources are visible and available to you, it's your responsibility to take action and use them to move your life forward."

From my experience, the clearer I am about my vision for my life the more the universe conspires on my behalf to bring my vision to fruition.
By saying Yes and taking action, I
attract helpful people and
resources in the perfect time.

When I was in college my Mom received a call from our dear family friends Senator Alan and Ann Simpson, from Cody, Wyoming. They were living in Washington, D.C. and called my Mom to offer her a job managing Senator Simpson's office in Washington, D. C. Mom was flattered and honored by the Simpson's offer.

She was excited, nervous, and apprehensive because it would be a big move for her. All her kids and friends were excited for her and encouraged her to go for it. So she said, "Yes," and moved to Washington D.C. to embark on a great new adventure that lasted for 10 years. She loved her new life, making new friends and connecting with many of her friends from Cody who were also living in D.C. It was the opportunity of a lifetime. She decided to Go Big AND Move her Home. She was so grateful and glad that she did.

Big change doesn't happen unless
you are willing to go for it!

My brother Todd use to tell his friends "Go Big OR Stay Home!" As a daredevil and risk taker, he lived his life large and true to this motto, which is the inspiration for my book title. Having a business with a home office gives me the freedom to live by my motto, which is a slight variation of Todd's, *Go Big AND Stay Home*. I have the freedom to live life on my terms and take the risks I desire to live an exciting life that is supported by my network. I enjoy the flexibility to invest my time and energy doing what I am passionate about in my life and business, while staying home or traveling.

Debbie Allen's Story:

I was fortunate to meet Debbie Allen when she spoke at a Women's Wisdom luncheon in Rancho Santa Fe. I was inspired by her heart-felt wisdom, passion, and expertise. I asked her if I could share her story in my book and include her in the Resources section.

"Debbie grew up in Gary, Indiana in a grass roots entrepreneurial family. Her father had an uncanny way of seeing opportunity where other people only saw problems. For example, there was a time when car thefts in Gary, Indiana were the highest in the country. Her father saw a problem. He also saw an opportunity to provide an immediate solution. They opened a rental car company, which provided people with a place to rent a car while waiting for their car to be found or replaced as a result of being stolen. Early on in her life, she started thinking like an entrepreneur working in the family business.

Always on the lookout for new opportunities, Debbie's father noticed the abundance of apartment buildings in town and realized that people needed a place to store their stuff. So he opened a mini-storage facility. He went to every bank in town trying to get a business loan. They all rejected him and said, "It's a fad. It will never work." But that didn't stop Debbie's dad. He believed in his business idea, so he and his family built the storage facility from the ground up. They poured the concrete and hung the garage doors. A few years later, their mini-storage business was bought by a larger storage company for a million dollars!

Debbie paid attention and learned a lot from her dad's business savvy and belief in his own ideas. She learned not to give up on a dream or idea that you can build into a successful business, just because somebody else doesn't believe in it. Who knows which idea could be your million-dollar idea?

Debbie considers herself the **Queen of Reinvention.** Throughout her career she has turned around companies from being in debt to making profits. She invested in herself along the way seeking support and guidance from mentors and coaches who helped her streamline her processes.

Debbie's absolute biggest fear is to, "Go out and get a JOB". Her passion and track record inspire people to create their expert status online. She reminded us that sometimes it's only a slight shift to quadruple your income. She has the eagle eye for business strategies and solutions to dominate your niche and become a highly paid expert in your industry. She teaches entrepreneurs how to create multiple streams of income and successfully market what they do to create a ripple effect in the world.

Debbie is living her legacy. She built and sold many million-dollar companies in diverse industries. Today, she is known as **The Expert of Experts** who supports her clients in developing brand domination around their expertise. Debbie mentors clients around the world, including small business owners, entrepreneurs, coaches, speakers, and experts, in many different niche markets."

Life is short and unpredictable. Don't let it pass you by. Go for it and let your vision inspire you to take the actions for your dreams to come true. Never ever give up on your dreams. Don't let anyone in your life invalidate your dreams or discourage you. Start by making your dreams a reality by getting the support of your network. Create your own **Success Circles** to tap into the resources available in your network, so you too can, **Go Big AND Stay Home**.

"Going BIG" is:
- Honoring yourself and the people and things that are important to you
- Celebrating your individuality, because there is only one You on this planet
- Tapping into that which excites you to live a wonderful life
- Living your life passions
- Sharing your gifts and talents with the world
- Making a decision, or better yet a cause for yourself, to live life to the fullest
- Appreciating who you are
- Taking a Risk on You!

"Staying HOME" means:
- Home is where your heart is… It's your safe haven
- Honoring your heart's desire and passions
- Living with intention and purpose to create your dream career lifestyle
- Plenty of vacation time without worrying about what will happen when you're gone
- Investing time in building your business from home or wherever you are in the world
- You decide which people and companies to align yourself with to grow your business

- Total freedom with unlimited income potential, flexible hours, and location

Blocks that prevent people from achieving their dreams are:

1) Not believing in themselves
2) Not having support
3) Not having the knowledge or skills

Sometimes we need someone to believe in us before we are able to believe in ourselves. Find someone in your life that believes in you and ask them for their encouragement and support. I've done this myself with great success. I'm here to pay that forward. I'm here to believe in you. Take me up on this offer at the end of this Chapter with a KickStart Consult. I'm here for you.

Take a stand for yourself. Inspire others to join you on your quest. Invite like-minded individuals to join your Success Circle for mutual support in creating and living the life of your dreams. Focus your Success Circles on anything from building a business, to getting fit and healthy, losing weight, learning how to invest, a book club, or creating additional income for you and your family. Let your vision inspire you to *Go Big AND Stay Home*.

What inspires me is the freedom to live life on my terms because I have a clear understanding of what that is for me. I have invested my time, energy, and money in creating my vision and mapping out my action plan with incredible coaches guiding me along the way.
Having a coach focuses your time and energy in a way that maximizes and surpasses your ordinary achievements. Being accountable to your coach empowers you to get out of your comfort zone and take the necessary actions to bring your dreams to fruition.

What inspires you to take action? Experiment to find out.

Finding out what inspires passion within you to go for it and take action towards your dreams is one of the best investments you can make in your life. It will pay off with a huge return on your investment. It's an exhilarating journey to discover what inspires and excites you. Inspiration brings clarity.

You may experience confusion and frustration along the way. Don't worry. That is actually a good thing because it means you are moving out of your comfort zone and stretching yourself. Frustration helps you discover what you don't want in your life anymore, so you can clear a space for what you desire. Accept where you are with dignity and grace and take action to get where you want to be.

Acceptance of all things whether good, bad, or indifferent, brings peace.

I live every day to the fullest. I take time to explore, experiment, and take chances to find out what my deepest desires and passions are. When I am balanced and living in the moment life unfolds magically for me. From this foundation, I set my intentions for the day on what I'd like to achieve or experience that day.

My intentions guide my day and attract people and opportunities that support me in bringing my dreams and desires to fruition. I am in awe of the synchronicities of life that unfold.

When I wake up and feel a bit off, I am compassionate with myself, because I understand that having a bad day once in a while is part of being human. I trust every day is leading me to where I want to go, even an off day.

I've noticed that resisting something can cause me to have a bad day. When I notice that I am resisting a task or project, I try to be mindful and explore the resistance by asking myself questions to get to the core of the issue at hand.

Questions to explore resistance:
- What are the tasks I have before me to accomplish today?
- Am I excited to do these tasks?
- What do I have to do but don't want to do today?
- How do I feel about these tasks?
- What are my emotions trying to tell me?
- Am I willing to accept my resistance?
- Will I take action even though I do not feel like it?

When I accept whatever I am resisting, a magical thing happens. I free up my attention from the dreaded thing and open the energy flow for a great day. It is during these days that I learn to have patience with myself. The lessons I learn are miracle messages that create the stepping-stones for building the foundation for my dream life. I endure undesirable moments and "bad" days because I trust where I am going on my journey and ask for support along the way.

Once you get past the resistance, focus on what you want to experience. Focus on positive feelings that energize and inspire you to move forward in pursuing your dream life. Shift your attitude to transform a bad day into a good one. Observe your thoughts and feelings. Be mindful in the present moment and go with the flow of life. You have the power to shift your energy from negative to positive. Being mindful and observing your thoughts is the first step.

Are you happy with your life? Do you wonder if there is more to life? Are you happy in your job? Let's find out.

Are you happy in your career? Find out by answering these questions:

- Do you love your career and lifestyle?
- Does it energize you?
- What parts of your current career do you like? What parts don't you like or enjoy?
- Are you miserable, resigned, and feeling stuck with no other options?
- Are you digging deep and being honest with yourself?

There are no right or wrong answers. This is a quick check-up to find out where you are, so you can make a plan, chart your course, and create your life vision, in order to start living the life of your dreams. Get the support you need to move forward to grow and prosper by using the resources, people, and services available in this book.

The best cure for the blues is an attitude of gratitude. Start a Gratitude Journal. For the next 30 days, look for things you are grateful for and write them down in your Gratitude Journal. An attitude of gratitude shifts your energy patterns to higher positive vibrations, which improve your mood and life in no time.

It is my hope that my stories inspire you to have the courage, clarity, and conviction to be you. The Merriam-Webster Dictionary defines courage as - *the mental or moral strength to venture, persevere, and withstand danger, fear, or difficulty.* Courage is standing strong in the face of adversity.

How do you gain courage? By going through adversity, experiencing the pain and coming out the other side stronger, clearer, and wiser. Courage gives you the strength to act in spite of fear and doubts. It empowers you to blast past the blocks that are stopping you from living a more fulfilling life.

When I reflect on all the major life events I experienced the year I launched my consulting business, I realized it was courage that got me through it all. It was courage that kept me strong when my brother called to tell me Dad was in the emergency room at the hospital. It was courage that helped me survive my Dad's death three and a half weeks later.

It was courage that helped me make one of the toughest decisions of my life and end my eight-year relationship with

Reed. Thank God he loved and understood me enough to give me the space I needed to sort things out for myself so we could reconcile shortly thereafter.

Shortly after Dad died Mom followed closely behind. It was devastating.

Courage and the loving support of my network of family and friends got me through the most difficult year of my life. I am lucky that I was able to be there for my parents when they passed away. I will treasure them in my heart forever. That year of loss and life challenges gave me greater wisdom about life, clarity about who I am, and what my life means to me.

Courage in life is so important. My dear friend Ken D Foster has taken courage to a whole new level. He's spent the last twenty years studying courage and the past four years writing about courage for his new book. I've been fortunate to have a sneak peak of his new upcoming book "20 Minutes of Courage", Daily Strategies for Highly Empowered People. I am incredibly inspired. I patiently await the release of this life-changing book.

As you go through life experiences that take you on an emotional rollercoaster ride from happy to sad, mad to glad, feel your feelings rather than resist them. It is our emotions that bring us to an understanding and clarity of what needs to be worked through. Feel your feelings instead of resisting them to be empowered in your life and business.

When I have self-doubt, I take inventory of my feelings to understand why I doubt myself. I ask myself questions to discover the doubt. What have I done that has brought me to this feeling? If I can't relieve the doubt then accepting "what is" helps calm me. Facing my self-doubt by observing it helps me move forward in spite of the doubt. Everyone experiences moments of self-doubt in their lives. Some people let it stop them. Others act in spite of self-doubt. Honor your emotions by feeling them and observing them, but don't let them stop you from taking action to pursue your dream life.

Even experts feel fear. They just don't let it stop them from going for it to *Go Big AND Stay Home*. Successful people take action in spite of fears and doubts.

I was fortunate to meet Peggy McColl, a courageous spirit, brilliant leader, and dynamic speaker who inspired me during a Women's Wisdom business networking luncheon in Rancho Santa Fe. I was in the thick of writing this book. Her talk reinforced my choice for the title of the book. When I had this epiphany, I emailed Peggy to see if she would be open to me showcasing her story in my book. She responded quickly with "YES!" We scheduled a time for me to interview her and add her story to my book! Here's Peggy's story of going for it in life and business:

Peggy McColl has written 11 books that have been sold in more than 81 countries and translated into 32 languages. She has also helped launch over 100 transformational books on the best seller list for authors such as Wayne Dyer, Marianne Williamson, Neale Donald Walsch, Marci Shimoff, Debbie Ford, and Gay Hendricks, to name but a few of her prestigious client list. Peggy is a master online marketer who has generated millions of dollars in revenue from her online enterprises, while living a balanced life.

Peggy has earned a reputation for being the gold standard in online book marketing and promotion. She is a New York Times bestselling author, an internationally recognized speaker, mentor, and an expert in the area of goal achievement.

She coaches other authors, entrepreneurs, and experts on how to make money online by creating their own products to sell worldwide.

I interviewed Peggy McColl about her business success:

Tracie Hasse   Peggy, how did you go from being an unemployed single mom to becoming a New York Times international best-selling author and sought after business mentor in such a short time? How did you re-launch your career lifestyle to *Go Big And Stay Home*?

Peggy McColl: I wrote my first book in 2000. I've had my company for over 20 years doing seminars, speaking, and consulting. In the 90's, I stepped away from my own business upon a client's request to work with them during the dot.com gold rush days. I was the Vice President of Corporate Development.

It was in alignment with my values because it was about developing people. I created a goal system within the company. They had a phenomenal idea for technology that was ahead of its time, but ran out of money before the product launch. No product. No company. No employees. So, if you're out of money all the employees go home, right?

Tracie Hasse: Yes, yes.

Let's go back to 2000. What was going on in your life when you decided to write your first book?

Peggy McColl: I found myself in June 2000 unemployed and I didn't really want to go work for someone else. I hadn't been looking for a job when I got that job at the dot.com company. I decided, okay, I'm going to get back into my business. It was a matter of starting it up again. Then I got this idea in my head. Oh, I think I'll write a book. I really didn't know what the heck I was doing. I was completely ignorant. Like, really ignorant. I didn't know what was required, and I am not a great writer. I'll admit that right now. You don't have to be a great writer to write a book, but I figured, how complicated can it be. So I read a few books. I figured I'd just use other books as models.

I've been studying success for many years. I really believe that if you want to be successful, find role models or mentors of success and model them, like mirror them, right?

Tracie Hasse: Yes, that's very true.

Peggy McColl: So I learned that it wasn't complicated. I figured it out on my own and I wrote my first book. I got it done. It took me a little while only because I was distracted. You know, I have A-D-D. I was a little distracted and then I got this brilliant idea in my head. I think I'll put a pool in my backyard. I just wanted to hang out at the pool. I realized I better set some deadlines here to get this done. I finally set a date to get the book done. Next I thought, now what do I do? When I learned what was required to have someone else publish or to self-publish, I decided self-publishing was the way I wanted to go. I had to get it edited. Put it into production. Quite a few months went by. The long and the short of it was, I wasn't earning any money, but I was still living the same kind of lifestyle. In fact, it took what money I had left to build the pool. I'm not really much of a saver.

I believe money is meant to circulate. A philosophy I have about abundance is that, if we hold on too tight to our money out of fear it will be taken away from us. I mean, we're going to lose it or something is going to happen right. I have a very freespirit abundance mentality. I spend money freely, knowing it's going to be fine. It will show up. I never know exactly where it's going to come from. I don't have to know. That's not my responsibility but, you know,

I have this belief it's going to be fine. What happened was I ended up digging myself in a very deep hole. I accumulated a lot of debt. By the time I blew through my savings, and my retirement fund, and all my lines of credit, and mortgaged my house, it was like, Holy Toledo! I ended up $250,000 in debt with no income. No income. So, I just decided, I've got to turn this around. Creditors weren't calling the house and asking, "When are you going to pay your bill?" It wasn't that bad.

Tracie Hasse: Oh my gosh.

Peggy McColl: I could see the writing on the wall as they say. It scared me. I thought, I don't want to go there. I've got to turn this around. I've got to start making money. I thought, we've got this thing called the Internet. I didn't want to be vacant from my son's life. I wanted to be fully available. My son was in a private school. I use to drive him to school and pick him up. That's what I wanted to do. I wanted to have the flexibility so I didn't have to show up at a job and check in. It was really important for me to have that lifestyle. I wanted to do meaningful work, make money, and keep my number one priority, which was taking care of my son. That's when I started marketing online. That was the day when everything changed.

Tracie Hasse: Wow! That's inspiring!

Peggy McColl: I learned marketing online from the best. I learned from people in the business and I followed through. I took action. It wasn't beautiful and perfect and seamless. There were some challenges, of course, but I started to get a really good feel for it. It's like a fuel. It's like you've got a fire burning, your passion. I had so much fun. I loved having the experience of having people e-mail me or call me or mail me and tell me what a difference my book was making in their lives. That caused me to want to do more, give more, be more, share more, and learn more.

They really created a wonderful experience. Yea!

Tracie Hasse: Were there times when you just wanted to give up and not finish writing your book?

Peggy McColl: Oh my goodness, yes. Totally, there were days when I felt like packing it in.

My husband is now retired. We have a waterfront property. We have friends visit that ask if I'm ever going to retire. I think about it sometimes. When we were sitting on the deck one day, there was a fleeting moment that retirement crossed my mind.

I thought, jeez, retirement looks pretty good. It's something that I never really entertained before, possibly I will.

The great thing about doing books and programs and anything that's digital is that it stays on long after we've stopped working or left the planet. You know, James Allen, Napoleon Hill, Earl Nightingale, are great influences on people even today. That's the wonderful thing about doing the work that I do. I suspect retirement is definitely going to be in the future. My husband and I recently bought property near a body of water that's stunningly gorgeous. We're planning to build a post and beam timber frame, beautiful, custom dream home there for retirement.

Tracie Hasse: How exciting!

What helps you move through difficult and challenging times when you want to give up, but you know you can't? How do you move through those times?"

Peggy McColl: Alcohol. <Laughing>

Just kidding.

Everybody's going to get knocked down, you know, at some point in their life or feel defeated. That's just part of life, you know.

If somebody has not experienced that, get ready because it's coming.

Tracie Hasse: Oh Yes.

Peggy McColl: I'm not saying you're always going to have adversity, but adversity happens for everyone. I find what really helps me is I immerse myself in positive stuff. I immerse myself in listening to great materials. I watch very little television and if I do, it is positive television. I get up a little earlier. I take action, even though I don't feel like it. It's probably at those times I really don't feel like it.

So I do something. I make a list. These are things I'm going to get done. There were times when I felt like I couldn't breathe. Like, oh my goodness, how am I going to get through this one? I say to myself, just breathe.

I create strategies. My whole book, *Your Destiny Switch*, is about switching your emotions. That's the premise of the book.

Peggy McColl: If you're getting the negative emotions, they're destructive. If you're getting the positive emotions, they're creative. So which side of that do you want to be on? You're the one in control.

If I find myself feeling an emotion that doesn't feel good, I can tell by the feeling in my tummy. Do the tummy test. Then you'll know whether it feels good or doesn't feel good. If I've got an emotion inside me that doesn't feel good, I know I'm not on the right side of that equation. I need to get back over to the yummy side!

So, I switch. I put on music, dance around, go for a walk in nature, take a nap, or meditate. I listen to positive stuff. I watch funny movies that make you laugh. Or, I help a friend. It could be anything. There's so many good things that you can do.

My absolute favorite technique I use is, I'll ask myself the question, "Peggy, what is it you'd like to experience?" I know I'll get an answer that is really wonderful and positive.

Okay, what's that going to feel like? It's going to feel great. I connect to the answer.

I breathe differently and at that point it's my responsibility to feel those emotions and that's what I do. I switch into the feeling. I act as if.

Tracie Hasse: At what point during the writing process did you know your book was complete?

Peggy McColl: When it feels like it's done. I'm ready to release it.

When I think about every book that I've ever written, I created an outline. I decide the book will be complete when I cover all the subject areas in the outline.

I filled in the content for each chapter. When it was done, I reviewed it and felt really good about it. I sent it to an editor then it was ready to go. I think that's pretty much the way it goes for most people, except for those that are absolute total perfectionist. They'll never release their books, because it's never good enough <Laughing>.

I don't really know anybody like that. I know a lot of authors who are a lot more cautious. But, there has to be a point you reach where you let go and say, "Okay, it's ready. I'm happy with it." And then, you have to let go.

There are people I've met who release books too early. They're messy. They're not done properly. That can be a challenge because once your book goes out there in the world, it's a representation of who you are. Everybody is going to judge you based on what they're seeing. You want to do your best work and have it at a point where you put it into what's called production. You want to feel, "Okay, this is great! I'm loving it! It's perfect! I've checked it, I've rechecked it, and I've rechecked it." You'll probably get to a point when you're writing a book where you want to vomit if you have to read it one more time. The funny thing is you'll probably never read it again once it comes out, because you've read it so many times. <Laughing>

So, that's the idea. I got a copy of my 10th book from McGraw Hill the other day. It's the complete edited manuscript. They want me to get endorsements.

Tracie Hasse: So for the majority of your books, did you pretty much take yourself through the book writing process? Did you ever work with a literary agent or a coach? You said you had an editor, right? It sounds like from your first book you laid out a plan and have been refining that process with every book.

Peggy McColl: Yeah. I would say I did them on my own.

Tracie Hasse: Wow! Impressive!

Peggy McColl: I didn't have anyone like a writing mentor or anything like that. I do that work now. The reason why is because I've learned so much from doing so many books, so I help people.

Tracie Hasse: Do you take people through your book writing process one-on-one, or group coaching?

Peggy McColl: Yes. When I teach, I don't teach a one-size-fits-all because I don't believe there is a one-size-fits-all option. I teach people to find their own style and find what works for them. I share multiple ways of getting your book done so people can decide how they want to do it themselves.

I like teaching online courses. I also do a total author immersion where people can come as a group and work on their books. I guide them through the process. They share and they get feedback as well. It's a really phenomenal experience as a live event. The third option is, I work with people one-on-one. It's totally focused on them, their format, and their structure.

I'm not always available for one-on-one's because of the time required. I don't always have time available. So, I'll put on my website, "This service is not available at this time. There's a waiting list. You can get on it."

Tracie Hasse: At the event, you talked about how 5% of it is writing your book and 95% is marketing your book. What are your thoughts on marketing your book? Have you ever hired a PR firm?

Peggy McColl: I prefer online marketing.

We're living in a very different world today than what we were 15 or 20 years ago. It's very different. People are connected online. We've got 7 billion people on the planet and most of them are connected on the Internet.

There are two-and-a-half billion people online now and that's where the opportunities are. It's so much easier to connect with people online. That's why I would recommend marketing online to every single author.

You've got to learn how to market, but not just market, market effectively online.

Tracie Hasse: And that's what you teach people in your courses, is marketing effectively, obviously.

Peggy McColl: Exactly.

Tracie Hasse: So, do you do any offline marketing or just purely online?

Peggy McColl: If I do any offline, it's speaking at events, but pretty much all the marketing I do is online.

Tracie Hasse: What percentage of your time is spent doing speaking gigs? Some people don't want to be a speaker.

Peggy McColl: Yeah, exactly. I don't do a lot of speaking gigs.

I'll go to events where there's hundreds or thousands of people there for me to speak to. People invite me. I tell them I'm not going to go unless there's somebody I can learn something from that I'm sharing the stage with.

When my son was younger, as a single mom, I wanted to stay at home more. Well, my son is an adult now and he has a son of his own now. And, I'm remarried. I don't really want to be away from home. I love being home with my family.

Tracie Hasse: What was your secret to becoming a *New York Times* Bestseller? Did you achieve that with all your books? How does that work?

Peggy McColl: It was with *Your Destiny Switch*. It was my fourth book.
It've done it with many of my clients too.

Tracie Hasse: Why did that book hit the *New York Times* Bestseller list versus the other books?

Peggy McColl: I focused on putting it on the *New York Times* Bestseller list.
It's the strategy that I teach and follow. That's how I achieved it.

Tracie Hasse: What are the top three things that you would tell first-time authors about promoting their books online?

Peggy McColl: Invest in themselves and learn from a mentor. They will be really glad they did because authors are very passionate people.

Most authors don't really understand the reality of the business and start blowing money on things that don't produce any results. Learn from somebody who knows how to get results. Are they teaching strategies they've used that get results? As authors, we write books to help other people and get our message out there in the world.

Authors have to learn how to do that. It was an eye-opening experience for me to learn about the 5% / 95% split. It's something every author needs to understand. It was a shocker for me.

It's like, whoa, wait a minute! That was a lot of work to get that book done.

I thought the buyers would come but they didn't.

Success is like that too. You think, if I just think success it's going to come. But no, we've got work to do. It's just the reality of the game. The good news is it's not crowded along the extra mile. There are very few people willing to do it.

I am willing to do it because I know what the rewards are and what they feel like. I really like it. It's really creative. I've created a wonderful lifestyle for my family, myself, and my doggies. They live a nice life. <Laughing>

You will reap rewards from being generous. Be generous with your time, ideas, and your stuff, and rewards will come back to you.

Tracie Hasse: Well, you are the epitome of it, I tell you.

Peggy McColl: Thank you.

Tracie Hasse: Generosity begets generosity, right?

Peggy McColl: Yes, it does. It really does.

Tracie Hasse: Did you have a couple of mentors that really helped you shift from almost giving up to truly *Going Big AND Staying Home*? If so, how did you meet them?

Peggy McColl: Bob Proctor was my greatest mentor. I met him when I was 19. I worked for this company that hired him to come and do a motivational evening that totally changed my life. I've been studying him for 36-and-a-half years now. I just love him.

I've learned from many other mentors as well. My son has been a great teacher for me. He's a very wise soul. I believe that children cause us, or invite us, to be a better person.

They teach us about unconditional love. Their birth teaches you about giving, nurturing, caring, understanding, patience, and love. My son's been a great teacher for me and still is a great teacher. I have so much respect for him.

Tracie Hasse: You really created a beautiful successful life and true leverage. Would you attribute that to the Internet? How would you describe how you use leverage from the Internet, people, systems, methodologies, connections?

Peggy McColl: Yes, I don't think leverage is one thing. It's everything. This week I taught three classes. One of the classes I taught this week was about establishing relationships, the value of relationships, and how to create them. That's a very important part of leveraging success.

It's also about having systems, strategies, methodologies. You know, like I've learned a lot about business from being in business and from working in the corporate world.

I started working when I graduated from high school at 17. I actually had two jobs, a full-time job and a part-time job. I've worked for big multinationals, small organizations, and mom-and-pop shops. I've had my own business for 21 years as well. I've learned a lot. I've been in sales, marketing, and training. I've been a vice president and on boards, so I have a lot of experience.

I think the only way we can be successful as an author is when we understand that it's a business and we have to wear multiple hats. I did a speaking engagement recently and made this point with a shark hat, an elephant hat, and a captain's hat to show them you're going to wear different hats.

You're an entrepreneur. You're going to wear different hats, you know. Sometimes, you're going to need to be the captain of your ship. Sometimes, you're going to have to remember everything. Sometimes you're going to have to be the shark and just get out there and make it happen and go for the sale. I talked about the different roles we play. You've got to be flexible. Sometimes I tell people my middle name is "flexible." You won't find it on my birth certificate.

Tracie Hasse: Do you have a team working for you?

Peggy McColl: I have a bookkeeper, an accountant, a web designer, and a marketing guy and all of them are paid based on their deliverables.

Tracie Hasse: Reflecting back on your career is there anything you would do differently with what you know now?

Peggy McColl: No. None of it. I'd do it all the same. I'm really happy with everything. It's all perfection.

Someone could ask me what's the one thing that's really made the difference in your career? It's practicing the law of GOYA, which is "get-off-your-butt."

You've got to get off your butt and get things done. You've got to move.

Tracie Hasse: In closing, what are your words of wisdom to *Go Big AND Stay Home*?

Peggy McColl: Keep investing in yourself. I continually take programs. I've got my mentor, Bob Proctor. I don't stop learning. I'm a student and I'm a teacher. So, you've got to always stay a student.

Tracie Hasse: Peggy, I appreciate you as a mentor, friend, and for being my true inspiration. I'm grateful for you living your passion and sharing your wealth of wisdom with the world.

Peggy McColl: Thanks so much. I really appreciate it. I wish you great success with everything, Tracie.

Tracie Hasse: Thank you so much.

Peggy knows how to *Go Big AND Stay Home*. She is living life on her terms and successful by anyone's standards, as a result of taking risks and action, in spite of her doubts and fears along the way. She has no regrets because she is going for it in life and business.

For me, *Going Big AND Staying Home* means building lucrative businesses that allow me to work from virtually anywhere - my home office, a traditional business setting or anywhere in the world where I have an internet connection. It also means working with like-minded, like-hearted, brilliant, passionate people. Those whose magical synergies result in prosperous businesses that we, on our own, would not be able to do.

There are numerous ways to make money. Do some research to find the best fit for you. Here are some interesting and worthwhile ideas to consider:

Money Making Options:

- Work with an expert to license your business model without the hassle and expense of franchising. Ariela Wilcox, The Wilcox Agency, is the only Literary Agent in the U.S. that's an Expert in the Licensing of Business Models. She has helped all kinds of businesses and professionals to protect their ideas and intellectual property and make money from their present business or service, from dog walkers to coffee kiosks, and every other kind of business in between. Ariela helps them leverage all the hard work of setting up their business and monetize their ideas. One of her clients made $200,000 in just two months using her method to license his business! And he was NEW in business and NOT profitable! That's the power of the leveraging of a business or service. Ariela's client sold 8 licenses in 20 months and then as he was preparing to franchise but he was bought out by a larger coffee company.

- Monetize your intellectual capital by setting up your own "Coaching Network" to create a distribution system for your products, free you up to have more personal time while creating a financial base of $240K+ per year. The Wilcox Agency is the only agency in the U.S. helping owners, doctors and professionals set up their own Coaching Network. The benefit of this system is you only have to mentor your coaches just one day a month.

- Ariela Wilcox's initial business model she developed 19 years ago, the 'Licensing of Business Model' was tweaked to use in the Coaching Network Signature Program years later and then tweaked again for Ariela's new program: **Design Your Signature Program In Only 6 Weeks: The Fastest Path to Attracting Your Ideal Client, Having More Time and Money While Living the Life You Always Dreamed of ... Right Now!**

- Start up a side business part-time, if you are an employee working for someone else. File a Schedule C to take advantage of write-offs on your tax return.

- Schedule time to talk to your Certified Public Accountant (CPA) to review business tax write-offs.

- Go to SCORE.org for business advice and mentoring. It's Free!

- Consult with a business advisor or LegalShield to set-up your company whether a C or S corporation or Limited Liability Company.

- Take action today to create a 2nd stream of income for your retirement.

- Use the Strategic Business Evaluation Checklist in Chapter 6 as a roadmap to make informed business decisions that you are comfortable with.

Imagine watching your life play out on a huge movie screen. Do you like what you see? If not, rewrite the script. You're the screenwriter, producer, director, and star of your own movie. Take artistic license to rewrite the plot with a happy ending. You have the power to make your dreams a reality.

It's up to you. Take a chance. Tune into and follow your heart. **Go Big AND Stay Home ~ Connect, Refer, Create Your Road to Riches**. Check out the Resources Section in my book. Make use of the high quality people and services offered here. I'd be delighted to connect with you and provide you with the resources to fill in the missing puzzle pieces for you to fulfill your dreams.

I invite you to take advantage of a FastTrack consult by sending me a personal note on LinkedIn or email tracie@ traciehasse.com with "FastTrack Consult *Go Big AND Stay Home*" in the Subject line.

Go Big AND Stay Home

Thank You for purchasing my book. May you prosper and be blessed in all that you do. I look forward to meeting you.

Cheers to You & Your Success!

Gratefully, Tracie Hasse

Ch. 7 Recap: Proactive Prosperity

Thought Provoking Questions to Think About

- How are you going to *Go Big AND Stay Home*? What does that mean for you?
- What limiting beliefs do you have that are stopping you from achieving your goals?
- What's stopping you from living the life of your dreams?
- Is there something you are resisting that's blocking your success?

Mindful Reflections

- When you are clear about your vision the universe conspires on your behalf and sends you the people and resources to bring your vision into fruition. It is your responsibility to say yes and take action to move your life forward.
- Take a few minutes every day to be inspired and experience the simple joys of life. You will become a success magnet.
- Big change doesn't happen unless you are willing to go for it!
- What we resist persists.
- Acceptance of "what is" brings peace.
- Make a decision to tune into your heart and follow your passions to flourish.

Epilogue

When I set out to write my book I could have never predicted all that this journey would entail. Through the years Reed suggested it would be great for me to write a book. I laughed and would say I'm not a writer. There was a part of me that was curious and intrigued by the thought of writing a book, however that was as far as it went.

Then I met Ariela Wilcox at Women's Wisdom. Ariela is the only literary agent in the U. S. who specializes in working with first time authors and oversees the writing of their book in six weeks. Not only that, I refer to her as a 'business wizard', because her 40 years as a stellar business woman have instilled great wisdom in her that she is ever willing to share. I had never met a literary agent. We connected at the Women's Wisdom networking event and made a point to exchange business cards and follow-up with each other.

It's a result of that split moment meeting and following my intuition, that I called Ariela. We had a great talk. Next thing I know, I'm in a consult with her realizing important things about myself, like wow, maybe I do have a book in me that's ready to be brought to fruition. This was revealed to me as a result of my being open to possibilities and doing a consult with Ariela. After Ariela lead me through her client discovery process, we discussed how writing a book could help to bring creativity back into my life again. By the end of our consult, I could see that it made sense on many levels for me to write a business inspiration book. I was up for the challenge!

As I said, I'm not a writer (or so I thought!). There were several key reasons why I chose to complete my book. To start, I was determined to honor my commitment to finish the book I had started. Working with Ariela, she coached me through writing the first draft in 6 weeks. As Ariela would say, the cake is baked. Next it was time to decorate the cake! Well the decorating has taken me this past year, refining my labor of love.

Writing my book was one of the most challenging things I've ever done in my life. It is not in sync with what I do naturally. It reminded me of my college days when I was at my wits end praying to pass Physics and Chemistry, not to mention my grueling Engineering classes. I'm at ease when I'm talking. Writing a book is not nearly as easy for me. Writing about what I do, I felt vulnerable... and still do. There is much to read between the lines and let your heart lead the way.

When I committed to writing a business inspirational book, it made sense. The idea resonated with me. I didn't know the how, but I knew the why. I had to follow my heart and it was time for me to do it. I wouldn't have committed to this undertaking had I felt otherwise. I've struggled mightily to complete this book. At times I've felt beyond overwhelmed and almost gave up on this whole idea.

I found myself thinking, how could I get out of writing this book. When I committed to writing my book, I told myself it would be fun. What was I thinking? Numerous times I wanted to give up and stop, even now as I'm on the final stretch. There always seems to be something to change. Is it ever going to be good enough? What is good enough?

However, I knew that not finishing my book was not an option. I made a commitment to myself and I'm here to fulfill it. What I've realized is that I'm not willing to quit. I'm a fighter and will fight 'til the end for what I've committed to and honor my word.

Epilogue

Over this past year I've had the wisdom, love, and patience of Reed encouraging and helping me along the way. The brilliant expertise of Writing Diva Deb fully immersing herself in my book to edit and polish up my book so the readers would enjoy my story coupled with her love and encouragement to get it done. The eagle eye of Donna, Julia and Jenny helping me with proofing, reading, and editing my book.

All the stories, interviews, Resources, the Foreword, and Endorsements by everyone in my book are all incredibly meaningful. Every person involved is significant to me. I'm forever grateful and appreciate everyone who has been supportive of me in my endeavor!

Infinite Thank You's to magnificent miraculous Manna who I'm honored and grateful to have in my life. She's a treasured soulful friend with the most generous and loving heart who has blessed me with her Endorsement. Her words of encouragement and praise helped me in the final stretch of completing my book.

I asked Peggy McColl in her interview with me, "How do you know when your book is complete?" Peggy replied "When it feels like it's done. I'm ready to release it."

The time has come for me to release my book to You, the Readers. May you enjoy reading my book to support you in achieving your dreams. Be sure to utilize the Resources Section with the wealth of knowledge available through every person noted there.

I have a whole new appreciation and admiration for all authors. This experience has enriched my life and challenged me every breath of the way. I must say it's been a roller coaster ride full of highs and lows and every emotion in-between. Would I do it all over again? Wow... Yes!

Acknowledgements

My parents' love, support, and acceptance of me throughout my life, gave me the freedom and courage to explore my adventurous spirit and try new things. Thanks Mom and Dad for making it safe for me to become the person I am today. Your unconditional love lives on in my heart forever. I got lucky being blessed with you as my parents. My brother Todd's zest for life to Go Big, take risks, and live every day like it was his last, fuel my fire inside to "Go Big AND Stay Home."

I am so grateful for the support that so many earth angels in my life provided me during the process of writing my first book. It starts with the love of my fiancé, Reed. He's been encouraging me to write a book for some time now.

Then there's Bodhisattva Bob. You fill in the gaps that no one else can.

Ariela, a literary agent and leverage whisperer, was the spark that got this whole fire burning in me to write a book. She told me I had a story worth telling that could inspire others. She guided and coached me through the process of writing my first book. Her divine wisdom kept me focused and on track to complete my book. Thank you, Ariela, for challenging me to leap out of my comfort zone to accomplish something meaningful.

Rayana T. Starre, a.k.a. - Writing Diva Deb, for showing up just in the nick of time to edit my book. You inspired me to keep forging ahead and finish my book. Writing Diva Deb is never at a loss for words and a brilliant business colleague. She contributed her magical way of polishing up my story, for enjoyment by every reader. She leads with love, care, and compassion. Thank you for showing up for me wholeheartedly, immersing yourself in my book and guiding me with your expertise. You are a pro and I'm eternally grateful for you.

Huge Thank You's Donna for your eagle eye in editing and expert writing insights that brought clarity to specific areas that I had not thought of before.

Dr. Manna Ko, I'm speechless and forever grateful for magnificent, mindful, loving, compassionate "You". Thank you for spending your time so graciously to read my labor of love. You filled me with such incredible love and reassurance that helped me to the finish line to complete my book!

I appreciate every person in my book, from family to friends, what I call my *Circle of Love*. It's because of each one of you that I was inspired along the way to keep writing.

I'm incredibly grateful for each person in the Resources section of my book. I admire your passion and commitment to the expertise you bring to the world. You all have a special place in my heart.

… and to the Readers, Infinite Thank You's for reading my book! Enjoy!

About the Author

Tracie Hasse is the President of Tracie Hasse International with over 25 years of business experience. She thrives on building relationships that connect people to make their dreams come true. Her diverse career path includes working with corporate giants like The Walt Disney Company, Kodak, and Tony Robbins Company. As an award winning Escrow Sales Executive, Tracie designed an innovative way to produce significantly higher sales. She was responsible for over 12 million dollars in Escrow production with her team.

Tracie's path to connect, refer, create your road to riches began early with parents who nurtured lifelong friendships. These early examples have lead to Tracie's phenomenal success and her exceptional talent for nurturing connections, growing her network, and showing others how to do the same.

She graduated college with a Bachelor of Science Degree in Construction Engineering & Management from Arizona State University and started her career as a Project Engineer on, *The John Wayne Airport Terminal Building Project* in Irvine, California.

Tracie is the U.S. Expert in Referring and Connecting with a specialty in LinkedIn. She empowers entrepreneurs and business professionals to expand their marketing reach by becoming more visible through the synergy of social networking, both in person and online. She shows people how to get noticed and take advantage of real opportunities to leverage and monetize their networking in a fun and collaborative way. Her proprietary Signature Program serves the real estate industry and other industries willing to invest in a unique path to increase revenue.

Tracie's passion and energy for life are infectious. She connects with an open heart to cultivate 'win-win-win' partnerships and forge strategic alliances that support and serve everyone doing business and benefiting together. In fact, she's often been called *The Ambassador of Quality Connections and Strategic Alliances*. As a result, she's been able to make smooth career transitions, double her income, and enjoy lifelong friendships.

She has a magical way of connecting to people by listening to what they need and want out of life. She looks for the missing puzzle pieces to help people connect to the people and resources they need to succeed and prosper. Whether it's in person or online, Tracie is always networking to see how she can help people get where they want to go.

Ultimately, Tracie realized that her heart's desire was to create her own business, travel with her fiancé Reed, and spend time with her aging parents. So Tracie left her job at Heritage Escrow to pursue her dream of being an entrepreneur.

Tracie's mission is to inspire, connect, and empower people through relationships. Today, she enjoys building business and networking. She is a big picture strategist who connects you with the missing links for you to create your dream career and lifestyle.

Tracie continues her quest to explore new and exciting adventures with Reed and their beloved standard poodle Ginger, in beautiful Del Mar, California. She follows her heart, growing and nurturing her network, while expanding her dream career lifestyle, as she lives from her motto, **Go Big AND Stay Home ~ Connect, Refer, Create Your Road to Riches.**

Tracie Hasse International

Tracie Hasse International guides entrepreneurs and business professionals to success with unique trainings and programs designed to use social networking strategically, both in person and online. Tracie uses her expertise in providing her proprietary Signature Program to business people that serve the real estate industry and other industries willing to invest in a unique path to significantly raise income.

Tracie brings decades of networking experience and proven business models combined with 21st Century social media and mobile engagement to help companies and individuals energize their network and take advantage of outstanding opportunities. Her mission is all about helping you connect with who or what will be the most beneficial for you, in real, meaningful, and tangible ways. Tracie Hasse International's Signature Program helps clients make lasting impressions, build customer loyalty, and jumpstart sales.

As The Ambassador of Quality Connections and Strategic Alliances, Tracie thrives on building relationships, connecting people together, and growing business. She is the Founder of Tracie Hasse International and author of *Go Big AND Stay Home ~ Connect, Refer, Create Your Road to Riches*.

Contact Information:
Tracie Hasse
Phone: (858) 356-2208
Address: 1155 Camino Del Mar, #123, Del Mar, CA 92014

Email: tracie@traciehasse.com

LinkedIn URL www.linkedin.com/in/traciehasse

*Note in Subject line: ***Go Big AND Stay Home***, FastTrack Consult

Book Website: ***www.GoBigANDStayHomeBook.com***

Peggy McColl, Dynamic Destinies, Inc.

Peggy McColl is a New York Times Best-Selling Author, The Best Seller Maker, & Millionaire Author Maker

Peggy is a world-renowned expert ready, willing and able to blow you (and your audience) away in more ways than two:

#1 GOAL ACHIEVEMENT:
An internationally recognized Speaker/Author/Mentor and an expert in the area of goal achievement training in some of the most compelling and strategic goal-setting technologies of our times.

#2 EXPERT INTERNET MARKETING & PRODUCT DEVELOPMENT:
Expert in helping her clients generate massive revenue by:
Creating valuable products
Building their Brand Worldwide
Making Money Online
Creating International "Best Sellers"

#3 BEST SELLER MAKER:
Peggy McColl has earned the reputation for being the gold standard in on-line book marketing and promotion:

Her successful marketing campaigns have been praised by authors and publishers around the world and are on the cutting-edge of direct-to-consumer book promotion resulting in the sales of thousands of books (not to mention millions of dollars and the transformation of lives)!

Her innovative and laser-focused work has been endorsed by some of the most renowned experts in the personal development field including:

Bob Proctor, Wayne Dyer, Neale Donald Walsch, Jack Canfield, Jim Rohn, Mark Victor Hansen, Caroline Myss, Gregg Braden, Debbie Ford and many others.

#4 CONSULT with Peggy for:
Her special, unique & intensive classes
Speaking engagements
Goal achievement seminars
Best-selling books that have inspired & instructed "everyday" individuals, professional athletes, authors and organizations to reach their maximum potential.
Total Author Immersion to get your book done….

Peggy's personal goal is to make a positive contribution to the lives of millions and she is beyond passionate about helping you achieve your goals.

#5 Peggy MENTORS:
Authors
Entrepreneurs
Experts / Business Professionals
Corporate Leaders & Employees.

#6 CONTACT Peggy:

Invite Peggy to speak live at your next event... To find out more: www.peggymccoll.com/contact/

Peggy McColl

New York Times Best-Selling Author, The Best Seller Maker, & Millionaire Author Maker

Author of 11 books including her recent Best Seller, "Darn Easy"

Company: Dynamic Destinies, Inc.

Website: www.PeggyMcColl.com

Phone: (613) 788-3200

Email: peggy@peggymccoll.com

RESOURCES

Resources

Get your networking off to a fast start and your business bursting with high-level professionals and industry leaders. I have done the due diligence and vetted these Resources for you. **Be sure to let them know you found them here in** *Go Big AND Stay Home.*

If you've not found what you're looking for, email me with your request at tracie@traciehasse.com **For a continuation and full up to date list of Resources go to www.GoBigANDStayHomeBook.com**

Amy E. Wright
Realtor Extraordinaire, International Real Estate Trainer & Speaker
Company: Keller Williams Realty International
Website: SanDiegoHomeLook.com
Phone: (858) 220-3768
Email: amyewright@kw.com

Angie Gange
Founder and Managing Partner: Helping People Create A Legacy...One Business At A Time
Company: The Legacy Group
Website: www.TLGPartnerships.com
Phone: (858) 472-7584
Email: agange@tlgpartnerships.com

Ariela Wilcox

Literary Agent, The #1 U.S. Leverage Expert & The U.S. Expert in the Licensing of Business Models (Business, Services & Medical Practices/Protocols).

Two Signature Programs (in addition to Licensing):

1. Have Your Own Coaching Network For A Financial Base of $240K per Year
2. Design Your Signature Program In Only 6 Weeks; The Fastest Path To Attracting Your Ideal Client, Having More Time And Money While Living The Life You Always Dreamed of....Right Now!

Company: The Wilcox Agency, President

Phone: (858) 259-3134 (Sunday-Friday 3-5 pm PDT – Mornings 10am-12pm by appt.)

Email: wilcoxagency@sbcglobal.net

Asha Mankowska

CEO & Founder of Your Favorite Business, High Performance, & Leadership Coach

Company: Asha Mankowska International

Website: www.YourFavorite-LifeCoach.com

Phone: (619) 471-6932

Email: asha_mankowska@yahoo.com

Barbi Wood

Owner + Designer + Stylist

Company: Considerate Done, Event Design & Production for those Events that Require the Royal Treatment

Phone: (760) 809-5097

Email: barbi@consideratedone.com

Brent Haywood

Owner: Full Service Photography from Portraits and Events to Aerial Photography

Company: Brent Haywood Photography

Website: www.BrentHaywoodPhotography.com

Phone: (619) 546-5109

Email: haywoodphoto@mac.com

Christopher Dilts

Co-Founder of Right Source Digital, Inc., Digital Marketing Strategist, & Business Branding Expert

Company: Right Source Digital, Inc.

Websites:

www.BrandExcelerator.com High ROI Social Influencer Marketing Firm for Clients & Agencies

www.RightSource.Digital On-Demand Digital Marketing

www.ThoughtLeaderImpression.com Fully Integrated Multi-Channel Marketing Campaigns & Crowdfunding

www.SocialVideoRocket.com Audio & Video Transcription Services

Phone: (805) 704-3451

Email: christopherdilts@gmail.com

Danielle Short

Luxury Real Estate Specialist, Top 1% Internationally

Company: Coldwell Banker Residential Brokerage

Website: www.RanchoSantaFeHomes4Sale.com

Phone: (858) 759-6502

Email: dshort@coldwellbanker.com

David Michail

Media, Entertainment, and Technology Counsel

Company: Metlawgroup

Website: www.MetLawGroup.com

Phone: (310) 243-6381

Email: david.michail@metlawgroup.com

Debbie Allen

Business & Brand Strategist / The Expert of Experts

Company: Debbie Allen International

Website: www.DebbieAllen.com

Phone: (480) 634-7691

Email: info@debbieallen.com

Donna Marganella

Freelance Writer & Editor / Marketing & Education in Wellness Industry

Company: The Legacy Group

Website: www.linkedin.com/in/DonnaMarganella

Phone: (619) 985-6414

Email: dmarganella@gmail.com

Dr. Roopa Chari, M.D. & Deepak Chari, M.S.

Integrative Medical Doctor & Engineer/Certified Biofeedback Specialist; Speakers

Company: Chari Center of Health

Website: www.ChariCenter.com & www.FastAnxietyHelp.com

Phone: (760) 230-2711

Email: info@charicenter.com

Dr. Manna Ko

Founder/CEO: Sought-after Speaker, Leadership Trainer and Business/Life Strategist; Author of 9 books including her recent Best Seller, "Made For More"

Company: Manna For Life
Website: www.MannaForLife.com
Email: info@mannaforlife.com

Dr. Steven Ross

Consultant, International Speaker, Practitioner, President / Co-Founder & Educator, Advanced Medical Academy, a subsidiary of The American College of Integrative and Functional Medicine; Author of "Curing The Cause and Preventing Disease, A New Approach to The Diagnosis and Treatment of Illness and Aging with Functional Diagnostic Medicine"

Company: Advanced Medical Academy, a subsidiary of The American College of Integrative and Functional Medicine
Websites:
www.DrStevenRoss.com
www.AdvancedMedAcademy.com
Phone: (858) 205-9735
Email: drross@drstevenross.com

George W. Hasse

Financial Insurance Advisor: Estate, Business & Family Planning, LUTCF

Company: Prudential / Hasse Financial Group LLC
Phone: (702) 647-9888
Email: George.Hasse@Prudential.com

Jeff Rogers

The Quit Whining, No Excuses, Get Busy Creating The Life You Love Coach!

Company: BrainStorm Success Training (Magnitude Vision Course)

Website: www.BrainStormSuccess.com

Phone: (702) 656-9888

Email: jeff@brainstormsuccess.com

Jenny Jantzen

Residential Realtor with Comprehensive Expertise in Property Acquisitions, Sales, Lending, & Development

Company: Shoreline Properties

Website: www.JennyJantzen.com

Phone: (858) 354-2710

Email: jennyjantzen@gmail.com

Jerry Conti

CEO & Co-founder; Strategic Partnership Expert

Company: Mission Meetings LLC, How Two Mentoring Calls A Month Can Supercharge Your Life & Business

Website: www.MissionMeetings.com

Phone: (760) 535-3428

Email: jerry@missionmeetings.com

Joe Loredo
Business Broker: Helping People Buy & Sell Businesses in California. He was a Consultant at Grant Thornton, Chicago, Illinois, and is an Expert in Accounting & Finance.
Phone: (760) 845-8273
Email: jclor@sbcglobal.net

Judy Ann Foster
Creating Fabulous Events for Fabulous Women
Company: "Women's Wisdom" ~ Woman Empowering Women in Friendship & Business
Website: www.WomensWisdom.net
Phone: (760) 703-9941
Email: judy@womenswisdom.net

Kathryn Holt
Feng Shui Specialist with Formal Education in the Classical Disciplines of Feng Shui, International Consultant, Speaker, Instructor & Writer of Feng Shui +
Real Estate Professional
Company: Feng Shui Resource & Kathryn Holt Real Estate
Websites: www.FengShuiResource.com +
www.KathrynHoltRealEstate.com
Phone: (858) 342-0968
Email: kccholt@gmail.com

Ken D Foster

Business Strategist, Intuitive Mentor, Business Trainer, Speaker & Author "20 Minutes of Courage" in 2016

Company: Shared Vision Inc. and "Stars of Courage 501c3"

Website: www.KenDFoster.com

Phone: (760) 515-9051

Email: ken@kendfoster.com

Kim Melia

Platinum Executive Director

Company: LegalSheild

Website: www.MeliaTeam.com

Phone: (760) 470-0300

Email: kim@kimmelia.com

Lisa Lockhart

Brand Marketing Strategist, Developing Highly Targeted Brand Stories that Build Enduring Relationships and Create Exponential Growth

Company: Brand Excelerator, High ROI Social Influencer Marketing Firm for Clients and Agencies

Website: www.BrandExcelerator.com

Phone: (678) 464-5472

Email: lisa@brandexcelerator.com

Resources

Mari Smith
Social Media Thought Leader | Top Facebook Marketing Expert | Facebook Partner:
Author "The New Relationship Marketing", Forbes Top Ten Social Media Power Influencers, International Keynote Speaker Specializing in Relationship Marketing
Company: Mari Smith International, Inc.
Website: www.MariSmith.com/traciehasse
Phone: (858) 215-3001
Email: mari@marismith.com

Marina Dunn
CEO, Director of Operations/Events: Promote Businesses Through Networking Events
Company: Bizz Connections
Website: www.BizzConnections.com
Phone: (619) 888-5510
Email: marina@bizzconnections.com

Maureen Pisani
Breakthrough Therapist: Master in NLP, Hypnotherapy, Guided Imagery, Energy Work
Company: SuperLiving360
Website: www.SuperLiving360.com
Phone: (619) 252-2253
Email: maureenhypnolady@gmail.com

Michael Stelzner

Founder and CEO / "Social Media Marketing World"

Company: Social Media Examiner

Website: www.SocialMediaExaminer.com

Michele Calo

Results Driven No Fluff Life Coach

Company: Michele Calo Coaching

Website: www.MicheleCaloCoaching.com

Phone: (443) 514-7833

Email: michelecalo11@verizon.net

Michelle Humphrey

CEO/Founder: Master Business Coach Where Bold Business Owners Come to Play Big

Company: True World Global Business Consulting and Training

Website: www.MichelleHumphrey.com

Phone: (619) 822-2602

Email: michelle@trueworldglobal.com

Michelle Martin

Principal; Boutique Marketing Firm Specializing in Media, Print & Digital Marketing Specialties: Real Estate & Education

Company: Mthree Marketing Group, Inc.

Phone: (949) 291-5123

Email: michelle.martin@cox.net

Maurice "Morey" Glazer

CEO; International Speaker specializing in U.S. Taxes & Compliance in regards to Foreign Tax & Creating Net Worth Using Effective Tax Planning

Company: Glazer Financial Network: The Pension Specialist, GFN Capital Management, Doctors Resource Service

Website: www.GlazerFinancial.com

Phone: (972) 385-0007; Mobile (469) 358-2818

Email: mglazer@glazerfinancial.com

Peggy McColl

New York Times Best-Selling Author, The Best Seller Maker, Millionaire Author Maker

Author of 11 books including her recent Best Seller, "Darn Easy"

Company: Dynamic Destinies, Inc.

Website: www.PeggyMcColl.com

Phone: (613) 788-3200

Email: peggy@peggymccoll.com

Rayana T. Starre

Queen of Quality Content

When You're at a Loss for Words, I'll Help You Find Them!

Company: Writing Diva Deb

Website: www.WritingDivaDeb.com

Phone: (760) 560-7447

Email: rayanastarre@gmail.com

Rebecca Massoud

Business Success Coach & Marketing Mentor; Founder SHINE

Company: SHINE Because It's Your Time

Website: www.RebeccaMassoud.com/gobig

Phone: (415) 505-1806

Email: rebecca@rebeccamassoud.com

Rio Tanbara

President

Company: RT Marketing: Action Sports Marketing, Sponsorship Procurement, & Event Planning

Phone: (949) 861-1846

Email: riotanbara@gmail.com

Roberto Monaco

Grow Your Business With Speaking / "Influencing From the Front"

Company: InfluenceOlogy, *"The Best Presentation, Public Speaking and Influence Program in the World"*

Website: www.InfluenceOlogy.com/thasse

Phone: (858) 205-9939

Email: roberto@influenceology.com

Ron Nash

Coach Ron Nash: Master Career Coach, LinkedIn Strategist, and Author, newest book "How to LinkedIn"

Company: JSA Global

Website: www.CoachRonNash.com

Phone: (855) 477-3737

Email: ron.nash@coachronnash.com

Sameer S. Somal & Marguerita "Rita" Cheng
Chief Financial Officer & Chief Executive Officer
Company: Blue Ocean Global Wealth &
Blue Ocean Global Technology
Websites: www.BlueOceanGlobalWealth.com &
www.BlueOceanGlobalTech.com
Phone: (202) 276-7589
Email: ssomal@blueoceanglobaltech.com &
mcheng@blueoceanglobalwealth.com

Shawna Allard
Intuitive Life Coach, "I Know What You Need to Know"
Company: Divine Knowing
Website: www.DivineKnowing.com
Phone: 1-800-KNOWING / (800) 566-9464
Email: shawna.psychic@roadrunnder.com

Thalia Poulos
Expert Professional Organizer, Speaker, Author "From Disorganized to Organized Beautifully ~How Six Organizing Personality Styles Got Organized & How You Can Too!"
Company: Organized Beautifully
Website: www.OrganizedBeautifully.com
Phone: (760) 519-9975
Email: thalia@organizedbeautifully.com

Tracie Hasse
Ambassador of Quality Connections & Strategic Alliances
Company: Tracie Hasse International
Book Website: www.GoBigANDStayHomeBook.com
www.linkedin.com/in/TracieHasse
Phone: (858) 356-2208
Email: tracie@traciehasse.com

Tziporah Kingsbury
International Transformational Leader, Relationship & Intimacy Expert;
"Revolutionizing Intimacy" Movement to Live Fully Empowered
Company: Soulful Relating Institute
Website: www.SoulfulRelatingInstitute.com
Phone: (928) 274-6787
Email: tziporah@tziporahintimacy.com

Viveka von Rosen
LinkedIn Expert & Author: "LinkedIn Marketing Hour a Day",
International Keynote Speaker, Forbes Top 20 Most Influential
Women in Social Media
Company: Linked Into Business
Website: www.LinkedIntoBusiness.com/cbash
Phone: (970) 481-8916
Email: viveka@LinkedIntoBusiness.com

Valerie Sorrentino

Meditation Specialist / Work-Life Balance Coach / Energy Worker

Company: Life Energy Coach

Website: www.FoundationsofManifesting.com

Free Gift at www.ValsGift.com

Phone: (702) 480-9646

Email:valerie@lifeenergycoach.com

Yelena Yahontova

Photographer of Joy

Company: Photographer of Joy

Website: www.PhotographerofJoy.com

Phone: (858) 260-0487

Email: yelena.photographerofjoy@gmail.com

Printed in the United States
By Bookmasters